ALSO BY BELL HOOKS

Bone Black: Memories of Girlhood (1996)

Reel to Real: Race, Sex and Class at the Movies (1996)

Killing Rage: Ending Racism (1995)

Art of My Mind: Visual Politics (1995)

Outlaw Culture: Resisting Representation (1994)

Teaching to Transgress: Education as the Practice of Freedom (1994)

Sisters of the Yam: Black Women and Self-Recovery (1993)

The Woman's Mourning Song (1993)

Black Looks: Race and Representation (1992)

Breaking Bread: Insurgent Black Intellectual Life (1991)

Yearning: Race, Gender, and Cultural Politics (1990)

Talking Back: Thinking Feminist, Thinking Black (1989)

Feminist Theory: From Margin to Center (1984)

Ain't I a Woman: Black Women and Feminism (1981)

WOUNDS OF PASSION

WOUNDS OF PASSION

a writing life

bell hooks

A Holt Paperback

Henry Holt and Company / New York

Holt Paperbacks
Henry Holt and Company, LLC
Publishers since 1866
175 Fifth Avenue
New York, New York 10010
www.henryholt.com

A Holt Paperback® and ® are registered trademarks
of Henry Holt and Company, LLC.

Library of Congress Cataloging-in-Publication Data
Hooks, Bell.
Wounds of passion: a writing life / Bell Hooks.
p. cm.
Sequel to: Bone Black.
ISBN-13: 978-0-8050-5722-5
ISBN-10: 0-8050-5722-6
1. Hooks, Bell. 2. Afro-Americans—Biography. 3. Afro-American
women—Biography. 4. Feminists—United States—Biography.
5. Afro-American women authors—Biography. I. Title.
E185.97.H77A3 1997 97-23506
305.48'896073—dc21 CIP
[B]

Henry Holt books are available for special promotions and
premiums. For details contact: Director, Special Markets.

Originally published in hardcover in 1997 by
Henry Holt and Company

First Holt Paperbacks Edition 1999

Printed in the United States of America

P1

in loving memory
of a life we shared . . .

in gratitude for a love
that gave me courage to write
a love that calls me to remember
and let the past go

what is lost because it is most precious
what is most precious because it is lost
—Amiri Baraka

Preface

To be born a girl in the fifties and years before was to enter a world where folks still believed that the most important event of a young woman's coming of age was marriage. Those of us who were not fantasizing about a white wedding and the man of our dreams knew we were freaks. We knew better than to speak our longings. From age ten on I dreamed of becoming a writer. Books were my ecstasy and just as I wanted to curl up in my tiny attic room bed and be transported far away, I dreamed of writing words that would offer someone else the same pleasure. The grown-ups believed too much reading endangered a young girl's future. Many of us were told early on that men don't like smart women. My daddy made it plain to mama that he thought all this book learning I was doing was going to my head—ruining my chances of a future. He could see clearly that I was already choosing a life of the mind over anything else. My problem in his eyes was not just that I wanted to be a thinker but that I wanted to talk ideas—to debate and discuss. And he believed if men did not like a too smart woman they really did not like one with too much mouth.

Mama seemed to accept the fact that I would never become a "real" woman, someone who would know how to take care of man and children. She decided for me early on that I would use my mind and become a school-teacher. In those days schoolteachers were always unmarried women. One never heard of them having sex or love. There were no children of their own in their lives. They had chosen a life of reading and thinking—a life that put them out of reach. Since they were not "real" women they were beyond the realm of desire. Passion we were led to believe was not in them. They were reserved except when sharing knowledge with little minds. Their lives were calm and discreet. They were constantly watched. In many ways they had to be much more vir-tuous than women with husbands and hungry mouths to feed. This was to have been my destiny.

My father was right. Too much book learning changed me. I was mapping a different destiny. Drawing from the life and works of Emily Dickinson, the Brontës, I knew that I could have both solitude to write and communion with like-minded souls to make life sweet.

When I journeyed to college in the early seventies I was surprised to find a different version of the same sexist thinking about women's roles I had heard in my small town Kentucky home. It did not concern marriage. It concerned the question of writing. In all my English classes, taught mostly by white males, there was a hostile undercurrent around a debate contemporary feminist movement had brought to the fore: could women be great writers.

Nowadays, almost everyone takes it for granted that there are great women writers, with the possible exception of old school patriarchs committed to maintaining a sexist social order at all costs. Yet this was a dominant way of thinking in our culture not that long ago. Challenging and changing this assumption has been one of the incredible unheralded triumphs of contemporary feminist movement. I vividly recall the heated debates we had at Stanford University in courses taught by women writers and professors about whether or not women would seize this new day and write our hearts out. The one cultural shift that was seen as opening the door for women to become great writers was the invention of the birth control pill. Often those individuals who believed women could not be the equals of men in the writing world thought that females would fail to realize creative potential because their time would be consumed by caring for home, husband, and children. Then there was the more progressive bohemian male thinker/writer who believed that one needed experience and adventure to write. Much of that adventure would be sexual exploits, experiences formed in the streets and back alleys, and through traveling. The single woman adventurer risked rape and/or unwanted pregnancy. And a woman heavy with child certainly had no place on the road. Birth control changed all this.

As way back as Virginia Woolf's *A Room of One's Own* the assumption that the heartbeat of great writing was not just a powerful imagination but a sense of the world led insightful women to urge that females seek adventure, grow and develop their minds and body, take risks so that they could and would "find the words to say." With the contemporary invention of the birth control pill coupled with a cultural movement toward sexual liberation, the female writer no longer had any excuse. She could roam the world, engage in random sexual exploits and not lose her virtue. Now whether or not women had the stamina to be great writers or even to write at all would be tested as never before. Our feminist women professors were encouraging their promising brilliant students to be daring, to explore our minds and our bodies to the fullest. We were the generation given permission to go where no woman had gone before. We were encouraged to chart new journeys, to make our own maps. We were inspired to act with the conviction that gender differences could not stand in our way; the barriers, such as they were, could be overcome.

In her course on contemporary poetry our inspiring unconventionally beautiful professor Diane Middlebrook (noted author of the controversial biography of poet Anne Sexton) handed us photocopied sheets of poetry. There were no authors' names on the work. Her lecture was on the entire issue of whether gender could be determined by writing style and content. Her experiment in class that day showed that it was not easy to tell the gender of the writer. I still recall the relief I felt that day. A burden had lifted. She had shown us that there was no basis in reality for the biased sexist stereotypes that were so often taught by other professors as fact. I left class assured that I could write work that was both specific to my experience as a southern black female as well as rooted in different locations and different perspectives.

Unlike many of my classmates who were repudiating relationships with men, convinced as they were that it would be too difficult for a woman to find her writing voice overshadowed by male presence, I was eager to find the "right" man. Once the anxiety about partnership was no longer ruling my life I was convinced I could settle down and pay attention to to what really mattered— becoming a writer. To strike up a partnership with a male who was also an aspiring writer was seen as sealing a woman's fate. She would always remain in the shadows. Those of us who rejected this logic idealized the relationship between Simone de Beauvoir and Jean-Paul Sartre. We were unwilling to choose between love and work. They had shown (or so we thought then) that it was possible to have a liberated sexuality in the context of a committed partnership of equals.

In those days I was writing poetry. Among contemporary poets, I worshiped at the throne of Robert Creeley and Adrienne Rich. I met the man I would live with for way more than ten years first at a Gary Snyder poetry reading. And then again at a reading where Thom Gunn read from what was then still a new work, *Moly*.

Tall dark and aloof, the man whom I had heard many folks describe as looking like a Benin sculpture had chosen to feast his eyes and attention on me. I was nineteen years old. He was only seven years older. Together, I believed we would make a partnership centered on our work as poets, our love of words. We would defy old notions that it was unproductive for a young woman writer to live with a more established male writer. Already he was seen by his professors as a serious writer. He was a graduate student completing his Ph.D. focusing on poetics. I was a determined undergraduate. As young black writers in a poetry world that was predominately white, we stood out. When we entered poetry readings we were noticed. Contrary to the concerns raised in women's studies classes and feminist groups, I was confident that ours would not be a relationship where the woman's writing would be overshadowed by her man's. We vowed to nurture and sustain one another. That was our dream and that was the way it was for most of the years we spent together.

No doubt what might have easily become tense competitive circumstance was soon mediated by the fact that I began to concentrate less on writing poetry and more on feminist theory. My desire to write nonfiction was totally affirmed by my partner. Years ago when folks would ask how it was I came to write my first book, *Ain't I a Woman: Black Women and Feminism* at nineteen, I would always share that it was after listening to me complain endlessly about the absence of material about black women in my courses that my partner urged me to write my own book—to tell my story. In those days women-only audiences critiqued me for giving so much credit to a man. Yet I knew the idea was his. And I wanted to give public testimony about this gesture of support because I believed it was important to give concrete examples of men supporting feminist movement (especially a black man as they were the group often seen as most sexist).

At that time I was not yet self-confident enough to think I could write a book. His suggestion was a gift I cherished and took to heart. He helped me every step of the way with research, listening to ideas, living with my heartache during the endless rewriting, and enduring the waiting years before any publisher accepted the work. In our life and work, we were both committed to experimentation, to a bohemian vision. In some ways I broke the pact of our artistic aesthetic vision of creating life as a work of art by becoming more and more involved in feminist politics. During the more than twelve years that we lived in the same house together I wrote two books. He finished graduate school, became a tenured professor. I also finished a Ph.D. in English but by that time serious conflicts had emerged—conflicts that did not go away. Our life was bittersweet.

Even when it became painfully evident that our relationship needed to end, I refused to accept that we should part. In the world I came from, folks stayed together forever. I wanted that for myself. I dreamed of being like my eccentric maternal grandmother and grandfather who had spent more than seventy years in marriage and companionship. I wanted us to stay together through thick and thin as my parents had. My writing life had taken root and blossomed in the shelter and sanctuary of our bond. More than anything I feared losing the writing discipline I had worked so hard to cultivate were I to leave this relationship. Unlike the French writer Colette, I never needed or desired a caring partner to lock me in a room so that I could write. However I relied on the solace of knowing that after long hours spent quietly writing I could walk out of my study and find sweet and familiar companionship.

These passionate years of mutual partnership centered on commitment to creative work, to engaging an aesthetics of living, were central to my development as a writer. During this time I created the foundation for a writing life that would sustain me and sustains me still. In *Wounds of Passion: A Writing Life* I return to these years, taking a critical reflective look at the experiences that most shaped me. Just as my first memoir *Bone Black: Memories of Girlhood* was not a traditional autobiography, this book of ruminations on the early years of my writing life draws together the concerns that women (of all races and classes) dreaming of becoming writers faced as a consequence of movements for sexual liberation and feminist struggle. The pressing issues of whether women could have love and write, whether we could be sexual adventurers and use those experiences as imaginative groundwork, and whether we could be the intellectual equals of men yet garner recognition as significant writers are all revisited here.

In those days all of our images of women writers struggling to find and maintain their voice were of white women. Simone de Beauvoir, Virginia Woolf, Tillie Olsen, Sylvia Plath, Adrienne Rich, these were the women whose lives offered us maps. Black women writers were not in the picture. When they entered the one woman whose legacy we most focused on was Zora Neale Hurston. Our attention was riveted by the tragic story of her achieving a measure of fame and recognition only to die alone, forgotten, and penniless. Feminist movement urging the recovery of lost stories brought Hurston and her writing back to the mainstream. Yet there remained a grave silence about her relational life. Even though there were murmurs that she had based her best book *Their Eyes Were Watching God* on the most important romance in her life, little effort was made to uncover biographical details.

Real-life romances between black female writers and black male partners seemed to hold no interest for the white women readers who were fascinated by the love life of Simone de Beauvoir and Jean-Paul Sartre or Sylvia Plath and Ted Hughes. Contemporary black women writers were notoriously silent about sex and love when speaking autobiographically about their relationships.

When their partnerships were talked about they were rarely if ever coupled with other writers, and if heterosexual were rarely with black male partners. Even though critics and fans alike rediscovered the work of the bestselling novelist of the 1940s, black woman writer Ann Petry, finding her alive and well living comfortably in the small Connecticut town of her upbringing continuing a lifelong romance with her husband George, interviewers did not highlight the beauty of their sustained partnership.

Given the extent to which racist/sexist representations depict black female/male relationships as always and only bitter or brutal permeate our cultural landscape in both written and visual imagery, the absence of alternative visions in both fictional and autobiographical narratives is alarming. Abundant portraits of black heterosexual bondings exist which highlight and even overemphasize the negative yet they offer little cultural understanding of the complexity of these connections. Clearly, we live in a culture wherein the political system of white supremacist capitalist patriarchy negates the significance of love between black women and men, actively creating a context where it is practically impossible for such love to be sustained. Counternarratives which offer diverse representations of the bonds of love between black women and men are needed as cultural documents.

Constantly faced with the paucity of nonbiased information about our lives as black women and men, it is both reassuring and affirming that we are witnessing a resurgence of interest in autobiographical narratives by

African Americans. Despite the growing popularity of confessional writing many works by black writers evade subjects still deemed taboo, particularly issues of sexuality. While there is a tremendous frankness in fiction by and about black people, our autobiographical narratives are often marked by a stern control and reserve. Often one leaves these works with only a limited awareness of the writer's life. It may be that the conventional narrative form of the autobiography lends itself to this obscuring of the inner reality and consciousness of an author precisely because it is usually so focused on the unfolding of a chronologically based genealogy.

Experimental memoirs have become the cultural sites for more imaginative accountings of an individual's life. Women of color active in feminist movement popularized memoirs that appropriated their style from pastiche and collage. In her fascinating memoir *Zami* Audre Lorde introduced to readers the concept of biomythography to encourage a move away from the notion of autobiography as an exact accounting of a life. Encouraging readers to see dreams and fantasies as part of the material we use to invent the self, Lorde invited us to challenge notions of absolute truth. Her insistence that there is no absolute truth when it comes to how we remember the past, that there is fact and interpretation of fact, has shaped my thinking about autobiography. While experimental memoirs by women of color often receive little mainstream attention and regard, experimental work by men, usually white but not always, is praised. D. J. Waldie's book *Holy*

Land: A Suburban Memoir tells readers more about the construction of the planned California community he grew up than the usual details of a life. Yet this mode of telling stylistically documents unique aspects of his past. Sesshu Foster's *City Terrace Field Manual* narrates in short poetic fragments the topography of lives in a multicultural world.

Even though I had begun the writing of *Bone Black: Memories of Girlhood* when I was in my late twenties, choosing an experimental form, I continued to write critical essays which included autobiographical material that was presented in the usual straightforward manner. For years I tried to find a publisher for my experimental work. I was told constantly that it would be easier for me to publish this work if I would turn it into conventional prose, telling a linear story, one that would move from point A to point B. Luckily, the current popularity of memoirs and experimental writing enabled me to return to this work with the confidence that it would have an audience. While readers from diverse backgrounds celebrated *Bone Black*, embracing both its experimental style and the absence of the kind of "tell all" tabloidlike revelations that folks often want from autobiographical narratives, individual reviewers were the most disappointed that they were not getting the "scoop" on bell hooks. They wanted traditional autobiography and as a consequence were unable to accept the book on its own terms.

Even though Toni Morrison's Nobel Prize should have forever altered the terrain of writing for black females, ensuring that serious work with an emphasis on craft and style could gain a hearing, it is still common for everyone, publishers and readers, to expect black women to write very basic conventional narratives. That may be one explanation why her success has not led to greater focus on serious writing by black women. Instead the literary marketplace remains more willing to churn out tabloid-like popular writing. Within the context of white supremacist capitalist patriarchy the proliferation of one style of writing sustains the stereotypical cultural assumption that black females by and large are not artistically able to create serious work and Morrison remains the great exception. Given this cultural backdrop it continues to be an act of resistance for black women thinkers and writers to write against the grain.

Against a cultural backdrop where black females have been reluctant to explore in autobiographical work the full range of our emotional universe, writing *Wounds of Passion: A Writing Life* was both daring and difficult. It is never an easy decision or task to write about one's emotional landscape. Yet I wanted to document the context that prepared me to become a prolific writer (the author of fifteen books). Again and again women ask me how I can write so much. Despite the success of feminist movement in challenging sexist assumptions about women and writing, the vast majority of females hoping to become writers still struggle with issues of creating necessary self-esteem, finding time, and cultivating trust that there will be an audience for their work. These concerns haunted me even long after I had published several books. And they often haunt women who cannot write as much as they want to write. From a feminist standpoint understanding the process by which diverse women writers make their way is necessary information.

Wounds of Passion: A Writing Life links childhood obsessions with writing and the body to the early years of young adulthood wherein I strived to establish a writing voice and create sustained work. As in the memoir *Bone Black*, I move back and forth between first person narration and third person. I conceptualize the third person voice as that part of myself that is an observer—that bears witness. At times I also use the third person as an attempt to distance myself from the pain. The inclusion of the third person narrator who has both critical insight and an almost psychoanalytic power that enables critical reflection on events described is an act of mediation. When we rewrite the past, looking back with our current understanding, a mediation is always taking place. I give that mediation a voice rather than mask this aspect of any retrospective reflection on our lives.

As in *Bone Black*, in this second memoir I do not chart my journey chronologically. I have chosen memories that bear upon my development as a writer. My intent is not to provide readers with every detail of a life but to share intimately the spirit of that life. Throughout this work I explore the impact a mind/body split had on my consciousness growing up. Clearly, many intellectually gifted women and girls suffer this split—eating disorders are one expression of that suffering. In my girlhood imagination, embodiment was feared as it was linked to exploitation and oppression. Yet later in my young womanhood I wanted to learn ways to accept and embrace the female body, to discover its pleasures. The desire for sex, the longing to reconcile these desires with a yearning to know love, were all part of my struggle to become a writer, to invent a writing life that could nurture and sustain a liberated woman. Fully feminist, fully self-actualized, I wanted to care for the soul and to let my heart speak. The word passion comes from the root word *patior*, meaning to suffer. To feel deeply we cannot avoid pain. In *Wounds of Passion* I write intimately about the pleasure and the pain to document the psychological and philosophical foundations of one woman's writing life.

WOUNDS OF PASSION

1

Not everyone goes to poetry readings to find love. She did. Growing up, poetry had been the sanctuary, that space in words where longing could be spoken. Nobody in her world understood. Poems came in another language. Nobody could find or hurt you there. She spent many a night sitting in a freezing kitchen before a plate of cold food held together by congealed fat reciting softly to herself sweet words—Elizabeth Barrett Browning, Emily Dickinson, William Wordsworth. Poems were the way to leave pain behind—to forget. They were a kind of suicide, a death. Her real self could drown in them. They were water to her thirst, cooling the burning sensation, soothing the red welts on her skin left by lashes from fresh young branches still green. Poetry made childhood bearable.

We had not been sleeping together for weeks. He leaves our bed and sleeps in my study. I lie awake in the night, the smell of another man's sweat on my body—the scent of memory. I want to tell you what my life with him was like. I want there to be a witness. I want to begin my story here in this place of lack—this place where I am seeking the fulfillment of desire—elsewhere in another man's house—an island man who smells of strong drink, smoke, and sweet cologne, a man who tastes of sand and water. Ocean is our meeting place, our watery bed, the breaking point. We meet at the water, lie together sprawled on huge wet rocks. Everywhere there is an open place we seek one another. We fuck where the waves come strong enough to carry us away, to carry us into infinity. We are too full of longing to remember death as danger. Death is desire—the place where there is no time, no present, no past. Our need for danger is no secret. Everywhere there is an open place we seek one another. I come home late at night refusing to say where I have been, refusing his touch, not wanting to go near enough to him for fear he will smell me and know that I am leaving him forever.

The intersection of poetry and punishment, a mind/body split, dominated her childhood. In every way her body was the enemy. Food did not interest her. She was too thin. She was desperate to erase all possibility of growing to be a woman. Her dream was to be a poet. Her earliest understanding of what that might mean all came from Emily Dickinson, her secret mentor and friend. She too was writing letters to the world, dreaming in isolation, reading and writing poems, trying to forget her body, trying to leave it behind.

4

The night before I leave he enters me. He helps me fold clothes, pack the car. He helps me the way we have always helped each other. This is what we believe in only it is not keeping us together. I lie beside him, sensing a stranger in our bed—a stranger entering me, taking me in the night to a secret place—a cave in the mountains where we will live forever. This stranger kidnaps me, captures my heart. He enters me, takes me to this place of no return, a secret place. We call it the heartbreak church. This is where I am left standing in the gap, abandoned at the altar. My gift from god abandons me, leaves me stranded at the heartbreak church, with no way to come home.

Morning comes and I drive away. Inside me I am still the country girl who never goes anywhere, the girl who will never be a woman—a girl who knows that to become woman is to leave the space of power. I go on without you. I go on without you—play the tape over and over again in my head. The song says *But tell me how can I forget you when there is always something there to remind me*. I am a woman leaving behind the man I have lived with for more than twelve years—a man who has lied, cheated, and hurt, a man who has fucked with my soul, ravished me.

I leave on a sunny day—the sky that strange particular California shade of bright blue—light piercing blue—a sky that like air in intense biting cold takes my breath away. Just as I am about to leave he hands me a mango—

says "When you reach wherever you are going eat this mango and think of me—remember our life together." I don't forget the taste of that mango. Its juices linger like sweat dripping from the body of a man I have always loved and have to leave behind—a man who fucks me in a fever, who wets me with desire through and through—a man who in the name of the father, the son, and the holy ghost takes me in the heartbreak church. He holds me underwater. The choir sings "Who's that yonder dressed in white" and the preacher's voice shatters the dark stillness with light—speaks in hushed tones "I baptize this my sister in the name of the father, the son, and the holy ghost." The taste of mango on my tongue. Wet rocks pierce my flesh. I am standing in the gap—covered in the blood of the lamb. The gift he gave me to remember him by—the taste of mango on my tongue like raw flesh.

She was nineteen when she met him. They met at a Gary Snyder poetry reading. She was wearing a bright pink dress over blue jeans. Coming straight from her job at the local day care she smelled of wiping the bottoms of two-year-olds, with chocolate stains and bits of candy sticking to her hair. She smelled of underarm odor and earth. She was in love with two-year-olds—ten of them to be exact— her class. She had read all of Gary Snyder's poems. He had led her to Buddhism—to Zen. This scrawny looking white man with skin like rawhide and a voice like twine made her think of chewing tobacco, of the loosening floor, of the braided leaves twisted by her grandmother's hands, of tobacco stains, of her brown skin—of home. To

6

her this mountain poet was someone familiar—plain—
and able to speak his mind. He could easily have come
from the hills of her childhood. When everyone gathered
around, she was too tired to speak, too worried that
everyone was smelling her funk—the sweat—the earth—
the scent of a long hard working day.

Being a child of god, I naturally believed no man would
ever taste my flesh. My body was god's place, the foun-
tain where the divine alone would drink, the temple only
the divine would enter. I will not have sex but I will have
poetry. I will not have sex but I will have words that make
me wet—that enter me, that like hands searching the
secret places deep inside a woman's pussy will take me to
higher ground. Words do this to me. I am young. My
flesh is still raw. My body virginal. They mark my flesh
with switches, cut fresh from the branches of old trees.
The freshly cut green stings my flesh, leaves marks—the
imprint of roots and branches.

   Mama's mother uses a strap of black leather with holes
made from hammering nails in a neat row. The strap
leaves its imprint on the flesh—tells a story I cannot hide.
I confess at the heartbreak church. I tell all in the name
of the father, the son, and the holy ghost. Confession
One: When whipped as a little girl shut away in a dark
room, I calm myself with words. I learn poems and say
them over and over again. I learn to enter these words
as though they are flesh, a body of burning desire that
can take me higher—take me through the pain and
beyond.

2

When you are a kid you ask yourself the big questions about love. When you see somebody with a scar across their face and hear grown folks snicker and say It was that if-I-can't-have-you-nobody-will kinda love. I was always deeply puzzled: How could you really love someone and hurt them. Or what about First Corinthians and all that poetic way of telling us love is kind and gentle. Nobody says anything about love that can lead to hurt.

As a teenager, she watched as girls at school would fight over a boy. She liked boys. And she liked other girls' boyfriends but not enough to be fightin' over them. In her house fightin' was not allowed. No one fought. Punishments were allowed and they were meted out with great drama and show of force but fighting—never. That's why when her folks finally had one of them knock down drag

*out, shoot out at the OK Corral kinda fights, it rocked her
world and broke her heart.*

*The fight started on a summer night. It was hot and
her mama was on the porch. They were sitting in the
living room watching television, when suddenly she could
hear the angry voice of their father, yelling at their
mother. They had never heard him yell at her—at them,
but never her. And when he raised his voice at them it
was never for long. But this time he was talking to their
mama and she came running into the house with him
close behind yelling and hitting. It was like they—the
children—were forgotten. And this grown-up bedroom
drama was taking place as though there were no wit-
nesses, as though this man and this wife were all alone.
Only they were not alone. The children heard the accusa-
tions; he was confronting her about sleeping with another
man. And as he yelled, and hit, he kept screaming I will
kill you. It was not the yelling, not even the hitting that
hurt them, it was the pleading voice of their mama telling
him that she did not know what he was talking about, it
was the sound of her crying. They had never seen her
crying. It was this sound that momentarily broke their
hearts. And as with all things she seemed to take it harder
than everybody else.*

That night it was as though she and mama were one.
Every hurt she suffered wounded me. When she wiped
away the small trickle of bright red blood from her cheek,
I searched for a tissue. When her heart broke, I felt mine
was breaking. Only unlike her I could not cry, I felt one

9

of us had to be strong. Everybody else had left the room. Even in the midst of her pain, mama remembered her children. She asked him if we could be sent to bed, that it was past our bedtime. And momentarily her voice was just free of all that was happening. Suddenly he remembered us. And turned his rage our way screaming at us to get our asses upstairs.

Let us not forget I am child of the backwoods, of wilderness, and renegade horses running free. I am already becoming a woman of my word. I know the meaning of loyalty. I know to follow my heart. I have to stay with my mother—to be her witness, to stand by her side, and if necessary to die for her. I stay. And not even the intensity of his rage can move me. Not even when he stops for a minute his persecution of her to say in that hating voice: Do you want some of this. I told you to get your ass upstairs. I was already somewhere else. In a world of the backwoods where the law of the father had no meaning and no power. I would not even look his way. When mama pleaded with me, in her best sugar and honey babycake voice to go upstairs, telling me everything would be all right, I was willing to walk away. Yet I found a place on the stairs in the shadows where I could see and hear and come to her if she needed me.

That was the night when he made her pack her belongings, every little precious thing, and leave. He kept telling her he was not gonna have it—she was gonna have to leave his house before he killed her. He went to the other room looking for his gun, for one of his guns. *And her mama called her brother,* the uncle we all loved best, to come for her. As she packed, his rage entered that space of terrifying stillness. The silence was broken only by her weeping.

I hated daddy that night. He forced me to make a choice. He forced me to choose between life and death, between him and mama. I knew I would have tried my best to slaughter him had he not left her alone. Of course that would not have been a wise action. It would be a wild gesture of heart-wrenching anguish. But I knew that there was only one life in that room that I felt like saving—not my life or his life, but the life of this woman, our mother, his wife who had been the one to sacrifice always for us. I knew we should lay our all on the altar of sacrifice and let her know that in the loneliness of this summer night, when her heart has just been broken, and the lights in her eyes are going out forever, at least she will know love. If she dies on this summer night she will know that no wrong, no transgression, whether real or imagined—nothing could ever change that love.

When all her precious little things were loaded in the car, he stood like a guard at the door waiting as she passed. Before she crossed the threshold to leave, he told her to take me with her. And mama still sacrificing gave me a choice to stay or go, letting me know it was all right if I wanted to stay, that everything would be all right. I left with her. Later in the dark at my grandmother's house, later after mama had cried in the arms of her mother, had been comforted by her sisters, I

11

finally fell asleep and dreamed. In my dream I reached
inside my body and touched my heart and it was all
shattered. When I pulled out my hand all the tiny cuts
were bleeding. All I could do was watch my body bleed
to death.

*Later when they went back home, there was some talk
about that night but it was soon forgotten. Mama assured
the other children, her sisters and brother they had done
the right thing by following orders. She, the crazy one,
had behaved foolishly. And worse, mama assured them,
she was hard-hearted because she would not forgive and
forget.*

I wanted to forget. I wanted to pretend that that night
had never happened, yet my dreams were always
returning me there. Sometimes in the dreams daddy was
killing her and I was watching. Sometimes in the dreams
he was killing me and she was watching. Sometimes in
the dreams I was killing him. It was hard for me to
believe that they could think I would not want to forget. I
could not forget even though I wanted to, even though I
tried. My dreams would not let me forget.

*That night changed her forever, changed everything
about her capacity to trust in the universe. Her bond with
the world of the everyday and the concrete was already a
tenuous bond. On this night it snapped. Nothing could
ever be the same. She could never trust that everything*

would not fall apart—it was then that she decided it was better not to try to hold on to things, just to let them go. Somehow in her child mind she linked grasping, trying to hold on, to her world shattering. After that night, and in the wake of that night, there was no room in her heart for jealousy or possession. She wanted no part of a world where hearts could be broken, and bodies could fall in the name of love. She had been a witness. And this she knew—on that night when hearts were broken, when lives were momentarily shattered, there was no love, save the love she gave but could not see. She was the only witness. And she did not see any glimpse of love's face.

I know that there is a way to love that frees. I know that there is a way to love that gives life. I know this even though I have not witnessed such love.

When we talk about living together, I try to explain things the way I see them. I try to tell my lover that there is a way to love that opens doors and doesn't close them, that I want to love him in a way that lets him follow where his heart leads. I assure him I will follow my heart, but never in a way that violates the trust between us. The trust is not that we will always be monogamous but that we will always be faithful to the bonds of love between us, that we will protect and cherish those bonds.

All she saw and suffered in her girlhood made her think these weird thoughts about free love and listening to your heart. Even as a girl she had seen the way the perversion of love could mutilate and destroy. It was to resist the onslaught of this destruction in her life and the lives of others that led her to think philosophically about love, to see the difference between love and power. To possess someone is to want to have power over them. It is antithetical to a love that need not coerce or bind. She was wholeheartedly convinced that if two people were open and honest with each other, committed, that their love would empower them to be just and caring under any circumstance.

I knew that he did not think about love the way I did. Still I believed I could convince him that it was important to let jealousy and other such nonsense go—to have faith in each other no matter the circumstance. After much persuasion, he agrees with me that we should have an "open" relationship. If our hearts are truly open to love we can't act as though we can control love's body.

To her a commitment to non-monogamy was not about a license to fuck around. It was a principled recognition that desire to be in the company, and yes, even in the arms of someone else, was not a negation of their bonds. Starting from love, the issue then was not whether or not to act on desire for someone else but first and foremost the meaning of that desire in relationship to one's primary bond. Would acting on that desire diminish the primary bond. Would it enhance the individual's growth and therefore impact positively on this bond or would it

14

lead to trouble and conflict. She was concerned with ethics and the meaning of love. While he could believe that she could accept him fucking other women (after all she was so strange in her ways), he was not sure how he would feel if she was with someone else. Both of them believed in the importance of individual autonomy. Her vision of their love was one of mutuality and partnership. Although he tried, he never really shared that vision. From the beginning in his heart he believed it would never work. He believed there was no such thing as "free love," everything had its price.

3

Abuse is always about abandonment. She knows that now. She knows what it feels like to be left stranded at the heartbreak church. She knows what it feels like to lose precious things. She knows that some things become more precious because they are lost. It all began when she was little and just starting to walk and talk and reach for things. When things she wanted were out of her reach, she would just keep trying. Unable to accept the reality of not being able to acquire whatever she was reaching for, she became violent. She screamed. She threw a fit. Silence, isolation, the small spanking, a beating if necessary, that was the way to handle fits. Their punishments seemed to make her more determined. She reached. They became violent. When the hitting would not work they began to take things away. And what better things to take away than the things she loved.

She loves cowboys and Indians. She loves guns. She loves Roy Rogers and Dale Evans. She loves Clint Eastwood, she loves to shoot. She loves to kill. She learns to shoot to kill, to shoot straight. These are the things her father and television teach her. She loves horses, the Great Plains, the frontiers. She dreams of riding a black stallion, of becoming an Indian, a renegade. They give her a cowgirl outfit, with only one gun because she is still a girl. She has a plaid vest, white cotton blouse, a blue skirt, and a holster with one gun. Girls can only wear one gun. She is dressed to kill wearing red cowboy boots. She would be happier to be an Indian, a renegade, but she accepts being a cowgirl. It is in the closet that she can come to her true desire.

One night they took it all away. They threw those red boots in the trash. They talked about it as necessary, claiming that her attachment to them was not natural. When they witnessed her heartbreak it made them feel glad. They had won. They had triumphed over that small hand grasping for things it could not reach. They had pulled her out of paradise, away from heaven, and brought her back down to earth.

Silly childhood memories. That's it. That's how they sound when I am telling them to him. Silly. I tell him the truth. I do not remember the big picture of childhood, everything comes to me in small broken fragments. Even when I piece things together, the pieces never make a whole fragment. There is never a complete picture. I remember that they loved to do puzzles, my aunts and Baba. I remember how completed puzzles awed me but I never wanted to do them. Games frustrated me, made me violent. Violence and will. That's what I remember. Daddy saying I had too much will for a girl, that it was not seemly, that I would not make anybody a good wife, that no man would want a woman with so much will. I do not know how old I must have been when they decided it was important to break me, the way horses are broken. We lived in horse country. I did not want to be broken. The breaking-in begins with isolation. The forced removal of me from the group, until I learn. I remember that what I was supposed to learn was how to be like everyone else. Alone listening to the sounds of everyone else enjoying a life in community that does not include me. They hope it will make me feel regret. I am not sorry. I am never sorry. And I am always alone—in that room—being punished. They are told to ignore my crying, to understand that I have brought this on myself. Everything bad and painful is me. When I look in the mirror I see pain.

Our father bought cameras. He was constantly taking pictures. It should have been fun but it wasn't. It was torture. If you did not stand straight or look the way he wanted you to look, you risked punishment. I was always punished. They always told me how ugly I looked, that the camera would reveal my ugliness if I did not stand straight, if I did not look the way they wanted me to look, if I did not look like everybody else. I hated the cameras. I hated daddy. I hated his need to break me.

Taking away the things that mattered. Food matters. I must have liked it way back then. I would be sent away without, isolated and given nothing to eat. Later I will stop wanting to eat. Then everything will change. And the punishment will be making me eat. I say no to food and no to punishment. I cry all the time though. I can't help myself. I do not want to cry. I am punished for crying. Everything in me is bad. And I am alone.

In my dreams I am always a young male Indian or a cowgirl riding my horse on the frontier. When they give me this cowgirl outfit, I'm in heaven. It is a dream come true. And then I woke up one day and it was gone, just that like that, my bit of heaven gone. I cried. I searched everywhere for the little red boots. I would not forget them. Years later mama remembered that they had taken the boots away because they were too little, because I wanted to wear them even though they were too little, even though they hurt my feet. I am sure mama's right. Even in my twenties my love affair with her continues. Mama is right. That's the way it must have been. It will take a long time for me to see that even if it were so, there could have been another way to take things from me, a way that did not break my heart.

Her heart broke not because things were taken away. They disappeared; that was different. It wasn't just an issue of loss. It was the pain of having something you love disappear without explanation. It was not knowing what

19

had happened that hurt her so. She was in such pain that it blinded her. She never saw what was right before her eyes. She never told lies. So she could not see the lies they told her. It was maddening when they all acted as though the lost object had never really been real, had never really been, when they all pretended they did not remember. They told themselves it was better this way—better for them to pretend that they did not know what she was talking about. They did not care that it made the world seem like a nightmare to her, like a place where nothing made any sense. They did not care that it made her feel like a blind person, that she could not see things that were right before her eyes.

I can laugh about it now. I can. I remember coming home from freshman year in college wearing this lovely coat from the twenties. It flowed with such beautiful lines. It was gray with a silk silver lining, found in yet another used-clothing store. At first sight they hated the coat, even though I wore it with mama's little gray hat. They hated seeing me in that hat. It was the way things always were. They told me how it ugly it was, how ridiculous it looked, how stupid I was to think I was looking good in that old mammy-made coat. When I awakened the next morning, I did not see my coat. By afternoon when I wanted to go out and walk I could not find my coat. They urge me to not be late looking for an old coat, just to wear my sister's coat. I do that. But later I want my coat. I go on and on about it, until finally I am crying and screaming. Mama sends my oldest sister out to the garbage cans in the back to get that old coat. I cannot believe my eyes. This is the way that they had lied about everything I loved after they took it away from me. Nothing had ever disappeared, nothing was ever lost, everything had always deliberately been taken away. Everyone knew but me. Everyone could see but me. I was blind.

4

Men look at me all the time. There are not many black girls here at Stanford University. My roomate Carolyn and I are into being looked at. We make quite a striking pair. Her dark hair against white skin and "nigger" lips, my lionlike mane of hair that feels like cotton and looks thick and luscious like a feather tick you could sink into. It's not thick though. It just looks that way. And when white people ask if they can touch it, which they do almost every day I wear it out, I just say sure. After they touch they recoil as if they just experienced an electric shock. They say, Oh, it's so soft. I say nothing. I think, So you thought it would be steel wool—something hard and rough. I never mind them touching or looking. At nineteen Carolyn and I are into the gaze of others on our body. We seek it. We are not into men, we are into men being into us. We are into being smart. We spend our time together talking books, ideas, longings. We like the idea of women as vamps. Contrary to what the world thinks, what the movies tell us, we believe vamps are intelligent women—girls who think the shit through, girls who are never mindless. We tell ourselves there is a difference between real vamps and the pretenders, the bimbos men see through. We do not believe they can see through us—they are too busy believing we are not smart.

Unlike me, she has a boyfriend. Now and then I see bruises on her body. She tells me it happens when they are drunk and having fun and things get rough. No man I know has ever been rough with me. Girl, I tell her, you better watch this rough stuff. Carolyn does not like the word girl. I explain to her that in the context of home with mama and my sisters girl is an endearment—a sign of intimacy. That I offer her the use of this term is a sign of friendship. White women, she tells me (like I don't already know), use the word girl when talking to a woman to put her down. She is so California. She does not even think about the south—about what goes on there, about race. Or she would know I have lived every danger of having a white woman use the word girl. She knows so little about intimacy between females—about friendship. She has no sisters. Her mother died young. I resist every urge to take care of her. It makes me sad though to think of her alone with no mother. I can't imagine life without mama.

I resist every urge to mother. That comes from

another part of my history. *Child, don't you be letting these little white girls turn you into mammy—you there to do your books just like them.* I do my books. And I do my share of chasing and vamping men—men of all sizes, all colors, all shapes. When it comes time to be serious though I mainly check out black men.

She was always troubled about race. Even when she was in high school, in the heart of segregation, she tried to make sense out of understanding the checks white hatred of blacks put on how folks could relate. She tried to make her own choices about it, choose by looking past color to what was going on on the inside. That was what she had been taught. But it seemed like nobody intended these lessons to sink in. She tried hard to create a balance inside herself, a place where she could respect the limits of reality, of time and circumstance and a place where she could choose. When she chose to have sex with an older white man, I was shocked because I knew she really had her heart set on a slim dignified-looking black male actor. She had been so into theater in those days. Her passion for the stage and performance just went away in a flash when she saw the way race limited everything for black females on the stage. He lived in a trailer with friends. She had no idea the number of women who had lined up to enter that trailer night after night. She just wanted him to invite her home. She was so innocent. And breaking in innocents was just his style. He was all about pussy with no responsibility. What he told her was No can do—

24

virgins are messy. The contempt on his face stunned her.
And in a flash she saw past the pretty features, the lips
like ripe plums falling to earth, and saw the hard cruel
vanity unmasked. She remembered what her Big Mama
had told her about looking past the outside to see the
inside. She decided on kindness. She found it in the not so
beautiful guitar-playing white man—a kind man with a
tender soul. It was hard to explain to the world though—
to her folks—to the crowd of young black men who had
pushed her on the street one night when they saw her
walking with him and had yelled into her face Nigger
gal, what do you think you are doing. She had thought
long and hard about that question. She had her answers
and they satisfied her inner needs but she needed it
to make sense on the outside as well as the inside. She
had no intention of lingering in something she did not
understand.

Unattached black men were hard to find—especially
someone she could talk to, explain herself to. Sometimes
she felt so strange living away from the narrowness of her
segregated southern black world. There everything was
clearer. Sometimes in this new world she felt she was
losing her mind, slowly becoming a stranger to herself.

Lonely at Stanford. Sadness soaks my body like that
moment when you are caught unexpectedly in a rain
shower and are wet through and through. When I feel
like I can't take it any more—when I am falling into the

abyss, I go to the pastures on campus to be near horses, the sun, the smell of manure. I read poetry to the horses—dream of meadows, of a place of contentment where all my dreams can be fulfilled. These days I feel as though I am losing my mind—as though mama was right that I should not have come so far away from home.

She is constantly sad—always been that way. Even when she was little. Her mama used to say that she had been such a fat happy baby then it all changed. She had only vague memories but they were different from the stories her mama would tell. She remembers somebody big hurting her body, being lost and nobody finding her but the bad man, who brings her home. She remembers that he wears the color blue, that he tells her not to tell anybody. She remembers the fear. Not much else. Those memories recede into the background, are overwhelmed by the pain that comes later when everything changes— when she is no longer daddy's girl—when she can do nothing right—when she is beaten. This pain stayed with her even when she went to college. Sometimes it threatened to overwhelm her—to lead her away from herself into madness. Poetry always brought her back home. She loved poetry readings. Not everyone goes to poetry readings looking for love. She did.

I come to the poetry reading after work—after the day care. I love children. With them I am connected close. Funny, I remember the day I met him I was wearing a pink dress. I hate the color pink. It was a dress someone in the dorm was throwing away. All my girlhood was spent rejecting pink, wanting it to turn into red, fiery and bright. Pink is all about submission. I wanted to defy. I wear a pink dress to show that I am willing to fulfill desire, to change. Work ends late. Damn. I am late for the Gary Snyder poetry reading. I come in smelling of children at play, the imprint of small unclean hands on my clothes—sticky smears on bright pink.

He noticed her right away. She came in with that wild hair and a bright pink dress boldly unconcerned. Every-thing he heard about her filled him with distaste even as it created the desire in him to take another look—to get closer. Something about the smell of that child-woman in the pink dress lingers on his skin, turns into liquid heat seeping through the pores of his skin like sweat. Some-thing about the smell of that child-woman in the pink dress chases him, follows after him like a harsh wind. He dreams about her—sees her as the little sister he had always longed for who will worship and adore her big brother.

The moment I see him at the poetry reading he turns me off. His name is Mack. He is cold and arrogant and aloof. He says something to me that is meant to be a put-down. I can't remember what. I see now why she says he looks like a Benin sculpture. His features are chiseled in stone. He must have a heart of stone and blood must not flow

27

through his brains. He annoys me. I worship at the throne of Gary Snyder. I meet some friend of his at the reading who builds houses. A big burly white man who drives a truck—who has known Snyder for years. I forget about Mack.

He does not forget about her—that high-pitched voice that pierces the air like a peacock cry—that ridiculous looking pink dress pulled over blue jeans and combat boots. He is haunted by the image. She enters his poems, his dreams. When she does not appear in his dreams he finds her in reality—observes her, follows her when she walks to the day care—watches as little child hands comb her hair as she pushes the swing or goes up and down on the seesaw. He watches her walking to class up the long stretch of palm trees. He never sees her wearing the pink dress. She wears long hippie clothing, print dresses in bright colors, dresses made with bedspreads from India. She walks so slow as though eternity is before her so she can take her time, never noticing anyone watching. She walks like an island woman, as though she is moving outside time—as though time is just another something she can make of it what she will.

She did wonder what it was about him that rubbed her the wrong way. He seemed to be judging her. That was it. She hated to be judged. And more than she hated being judged, she hated to be found wanting. Deep inside she felt he had found her wanting in some way. It returned

*her to that familiar feeling of unbelonging in childhood—
of not being a part of the group, of feeling somehow
always outside. She felt he could see all her shortcomings
and judged her by them. Time passes. She has a fleeting
romance with Garcia, a young Mestizo born in Mexico
and raised in Los Angeles. He worked at the day care.
After she slept with him there was never the same ease
between them. She regretted the loss of that ease—the
passion that took the comfort away.*

I have difficulty with loss—with letting go. I understand
this part of me so well I protect it. I do not allow my heart
to attach itself. Even without deep attachment loss
threatens to overwhelm. Look at how it was with me and
the Indian—how many times I went searching for him to
see if we could talk. It never happened—the conversation
that would make sense of what happened between us. *All
that she was allowed to know was that everything
changed.* We still worked together at the day care only it
was never the same.

*She meets Mack again at yet another poetry reading. This
time it's Thom Gunn who reads from* Moly. *As usual
there is a party after the reading. She hates parties but
she goes. Mack comes late just when she is leaving, tells
her he's been eating peyote all day—trying to find new
visions to give his words. He does not know yet how much
drugs will frighten her. He believes he can show her
things, take her places she has not been before—make her*

into the little sister he never had—the girl of his dreams. They agreed to meet that night. He will come to her place.

Her place was constantly changing. She was always moving—always finding something that made where she was unbearable. Looked at now, it was clearly always about displacement. She moved. First it was away from her roommate. It was into a room of her own across the hall—an unbearably tiny room—but all hers. Privacy was a new and rare thing for her, having grown up in a small house with her mama and daddy, her one brother and five sisters. After moving into that tiny room, she sat on the bed, really a small mattress on the floor, and thought about the fact that she had never been alone a day in her life before this room. It was certainly a new beginning. Being alone in the room was not enough privacy. She could still hear the sound of the hallways, doors banging, water running, silly yelling and screaming all night long. It was all so new and alien to her. No one in her family had talked about what college would be like— she had no references—no way to understand.

Fundamentally, I had no way to understand living among strangers. Nothing personal I had ever done growing up was outside the realm of the familiar. It created so much uncertainty. I hated showering with strangers in the room. I would wake before dawn to wash myself—to be in the silence of cleaning—to be where no one's eyes could look at me. It tormented me most to hear strange sounds all the time, to have lights on. I wanted dark and

30

stillness—something familiar that would remind me of home—that would let me rest. I found a home for myself—three tiny attic rooms—a small living room, a really small kitchen, and a bedroom.

After the Thom Gunn reading the two of them agreed to meet. Mack came to her place bringing poems. She fed him her favorite southern foods—hot water corn bread, cabbage, and tomatoes. She wanted to know about the woman in the background, the one she could hear talking. He told her the woman he lived with was a real Gypsy. Her name was lovely and mysterious—not real though. Only she didn't know this at the time. Real name or not Mack and this white woman were living together— in an open relationship though—or so he said.

All that I had learned about love between women and men growing up only made it clear to me that this kind of loving was not for me. I saw so much jealousy—the kind that hurt—the shoot and cut kind—the *if i can't have you nobody can* kind. Her daddy was a jealous man. And when that jealous rage overtook him just one time, it made their whole world ugly and violent. It was never really clear what had happened, if anything—only that he could not bear the thought of it—that it made him want to kill.

She sensed the danger of this kinda love and didn't want it. She did not want to be owned, possessed, fought over. She entered her teens believing it was best to let folks

31

have what they need in life—not to try to hold or bind them—just let them have what they need without the hurt. Her granddaddy talked to her about these things when they sat together. She never asked him why he had his own room, why he and her grandmama married more than seventy years slept apart. He did say that it was just good to have space that was your own, that you could live in however you liked. What he didn't say she learned from Felix an old friend of the family—Felix the hobo who jumped trains—the man on the run. She could ask and he could tell. And so she learned and thought about what she learned. And she came up with no space for owning, for binding another.

I have always had theories in my head. I spent time imagining what it would be like to take the theories out of my head and live them. I had my thinking about free love. With Lee, the guitar-playing bluegrass man, we just let each other be. We were into letting each other go— to being kind. No jealousy, no unnecessary pain. No jealousy—no lies. Lying was at the heart of all acts of betrayal. And so I understood that to tell the truth was the only way to make loving somebody a sane thing. I didn't mind him living with the Gypsy woman. She had nothing to do with us. At least not in the beginning. He wanted to have sex the first time he entered those small rooms. I read him poems. A poem came in the mail unsigned, ending with the line *her voice if at all she spoke it sang.* I am finding my voice—the poems I want to write are coming to me. Love too has found me, discovered these three small attic rooms.

I need the truth to see clearly. Lies make me dizzy, make me feel as though I am falling, toppling over with no way to regain balance. I don't know how to tell them don't lie to me, just don't lie to me. They love to see me toppling over, falling into the madness they have decreed is my destiny. Every year of my childhood I can remember them telling me I am crazy, that I will end up in a mental institution, that no one will visit me there. Just the thought of all that isolation slaughters something within me, I am ready and willing to obey. I am willing to accept the loss of everything I love if it means I won't be crazy. Lies make me crazy. Don't lie to me.

He lied to her though. And really that was the beginning of the end.

Maybe that is why no one wanted me to see her, to talk to her—the Gypsy woman—the woman he had been living with all that time. They were all more worldly than me. They knew she would tell me her story. I believe that I can see into her heart. When I look inside I see nothing corrupt there just a feeling of pain and desperation. That is how I know she is telling me the truth. She tells me they have never had an open relationship, never agreed that they could be with someone else. I believed him when he told me that. I trusted him without trying to see into his heart. I trusted him because I was desperate.

There was a tenderness between her and me. We understood each other, the longing. I admit. She was like a child. Like so many white women I had come across. She did not seem to understand that you could not make things right by holding on to people when they wanted you to let go. She seemed like a child to me because she believed that love would make everything easy—simple. I come back from walking her to the bus station, sit in that room full of shadows. Lies make me crazy. My head is spinning but I am determined to keep still, to let the moment pass, not to let these lies shatter me.

Her desperation is so intense. She has been wanting to end her life for years now. The first time—she was sixteen. She did not do anything like slit her wrists, take sleeping pills, or hold a loaded gun to her chest. She dreamed of walking up to Blue Lake, of surrendering herself to the waterfall and the rocks. She dreamed of letting her body go there, letting it be swept away by currents too strong to fight. It was the desire not to stand on the edge of the cliff, not to fall off that was leading her to him. She needed him to push death back—to keep her from being swept away.

When I looked into my heart on that still rainy night, I saw fierce waves gray green, a sea of pain engulfing me. I saw myself drowning. And the hand he held out to me was the only rescue in sight. He was holding out his hand to me. And even though he had told me lies, I could not turn away. That hand was all that stood between me and death. I grasped it.

He did not believe in truth. He believed everything was relative. She lived too much in a world of black and white. Lies were necessary. Why couldn't she see that. Why couldn't she see that the world would be a crazy place if everyone walked around trying to tell the truth. And anyway to give up lying would be like surrendering your only real weapon to the enemy. He liked lying to her. It was a way to test her innocence. He liked seeing that he could rock her world, shatter everything, just by telling a lie.

She thinks it is enough to forgive. She thinks that everything that can be understood can be forgiven. That's how she survived her childhood, by taking every little thing apart, examining it, and understanding the reasons. She forgives him. It is only the closeness she feels toward him that changes. She moves a little farther away.

There is never any need to tell lies. There is nothing we cannot openly share. I tell you everything. And if there is something I am forgetting then you have only to ask me to know. When love is real, there is no need to lie. Everything can always be forgiven. There is no need to lie.

They make promises to tell each other the truth, the hard truths not just the easy ones. They promise to share when they feel the longing for someone else's love. They promise to share the truth of their desire. She thinks she can keep away the pain of childhood, of endless betrayal if she just creates a space where the truth is told. She thinks the problem is not that we transgress but that we seek to hide transgression. She tells the truth even when it hurts.

He hates her honesty. It stands before him like a judge, who listens to his testimony, and hears the sounds behind his words, the story he is not telling. He admires her courage but he hates her commitment to truth telling. To him the truth is a raw uncooked thing, like a slab of red meat on a table, laid out like a dead body naked and cold. To him the truth is never as powerful as a lie. Truth is something you have to let go, but you can hold on to a lie. It can shelter and comfort you. The truth is never comforting; it always disturbs. He tries to tell the truth for her sake. He knows that she needs the truth to be sane, that lies drive her crazy.

Nobody told me leaving home would be like this—that the world would be so full of lies. I thought that when I left home, I would leave the lies behind, that I would make a whole new world for myself full of clarity and light. The truth is the light. This was the way I saved myself when all around me everything was closing in. Whenever bad things happened I would tell myself Look for the truth. Be guided by the truth. Never be so attached to someone that you are not willing to see the truth. I looked at mama and saw her truth. I looked at daddy and saw his truth. It did not matter that I had to look past all the lies to get to their truth. In the end it was seeing past all the lying moments that made it possible to find a fragment of light to cling to.

I am drowning, and need to be rescued. I reach for his hand. He gives me his hand. And we are one. He leads out of the dark wilderness of longing I am trapped in and I am eternally grateful. He has saved my life. It is easy to forgive him his lies. I owe him my life. I want to become a writer who can tell it like it is, who can speak the truth.

He wants only to make words do his bidding. He is willing to stray from the path of truth to reach that final beauty. They have a different relationship to language. She likes to peel away the layers, to strip everything, to leave words naked. He likes to dress words up, to cover them in layers and layers of language. He likes to obscure the truth. She likes to expose it. In their own ways they are both interested in the archaeology of the "lie."

5

In her childhood she learned to leave behind pain by reading books. Sometimes they took the books away—too many words, too much pleasure. She turned to poetry. Words to learn by heart—to say over and over again in the dark.

I learned poems, saying them over and over again—poems to take the pain away. The words linger—caress me like hands on my flesh. I call them out of me whenever pain comes. I call them: "the world is too much with us; late and soon, Getting and spending, we lay waste our powers." I call them out of me: "how do I love thee? Let me count the ways. I love thee to the depth and breadth and height My soul can reach." I call them: "Márgarét, áre you grieving Over Goldengrove unleaving? Leáves, líke the things of man, you With your fresh thoughts care for, can you?" I call: "nothing can bring back the hour Of splendor in the grass, of glory in the flower; We will grieve not." I call them: "the Soul selects her own Society—Then—shuts the Door." In my teenage years I hear voices. I am writing poetry. My mythic mother is Emily Dickinson. Her womb is a space of words where seeds of me enter and grow. I am born again—lost to the father, the son, and the holy ghost.

She arrived at college confident that she was a poet. She was not searching for an identity. She was not even searching for love. She knew she was a poet. Writing classes were a way to learn craft. She hopes to spend a lifetime writing words that will take her to a space where there is no pain. This is the fantasy that drives her—this longing to be released from pain.

I arrive at college confident that I am a poet. I want to learn craft. I end up taking creative writing classes with white male professors who cannot hear my words, who dream of pushing hard dicks into the bodies of young tight raw flesh while we are reading poems. I want them to find words. They hope to enter a space without words, to enter flesh that is young and tight and raw—flesh that can be pushed and forced—that can be separated.

She comes to college understanding that something happened in childhood that made her separate mind and body. She comes to college imagining it to be a space where all the broken bits and pieces of her heart will come together. Learning will let her be whole. In poetry she will seek the union of mind and body. In the body of poets, older and more experienced, she will seek to find herself. To be heard as a poet she must be seen. To be seen she must be sexual.

I am ready for words—for poems—for sex. Eager to eat the flesh of men, to taste and see. I read poems every day. Words call me. I will not shy away from Wallace Stevens's "Peter Quince at the Clavier." It calls me. I obey: "just as my fingers on these keys Make music, so the selfsame sounds On my spirit make a music, too. Music is feeling, then, not sound; And thus it is that what I feel, Here in this room, desiring you." Poetry sustains me. Sex does not. Sex fails to capture me the way words do.

In her imagination race and sex are intimately bound. Like two hands, two feet, two eyes—one did not exist without the other. Young black girls in the south learn it early—learn sex by being told to stay away from men. There is a silence about sex in every house but not when it comes to warning black girls to stay away from strange white men with strange desires no one black could understand.

She remembers the day they all heard. A strange white man was driving around the black side of town buck naked. He wanted us to see him—to come close and look at him. A stranger in a car wanting to be seen—wanting to pay black child bodies not to run away—not to tell. She

40

remembers because they were not allowed to wander around outside. She remembers grown black men arming themselves, searching the streets, ready to protect their own.

Memories of being told to stay away from white men stayed with me. But like those metal detectors, I learned early which white men were low-down—looking for hot black pussy—looking to get some from anything black wearing a skirt, and those white men who minded their own business, who could look at you without sex on their mind. If only I had a dollar for every white man that tried to lure us to take a ride. Growing up southern was to know race and sex were always mixed—always present even without the "other." Everything about race had shaped black desire. We had to learn it young cause southern white men couldn't tell the difference between girl and woman—not if her color was black. And everything black could be bought, had, taken, owned. Nothing that I knew about white men kept me from staring into the face of their desire and choosing. I wanted to look past race to find me a man who would do with my body what I wanted him to do. The first man I chose was white—not a pretty man on the outside but his soul was pretty. With him I learned to take my time with desire.

She met that strange-looking white man in a bar hanging out with poets and musicians. In those days she pretended to play the guitar and sing. Believe me, girlfriend could talk up a storm but she did not have no singing

41

*voice. It was midnight one time. They were walking and it
began to rain. They stood in a doorway—her and this
white man—and she listened while he played bluegrass
music on his guitar. He sang her favorite* warmth is just a
word—*she needs something else that she can feel. They
went to his place, ate brown rice, listened to music. He
dropped acid. She sipped tea. When she left the state they
promised to keep in touch. He wrote letters—sent her
Valentine cards for years.*

I had no idea what the west would be like when I decided
to come to Stanford University. I had never been on a
city bus, an escalator, an airplane, but I was going there.
Mama had wanted me to go to school closer to home.
Daddy who had not spoken a word to me had just said
no. I listened. And then I disobeyed. I had to get far away
from home—far away from the south—far enough to find
myself. When I got there nothing was the same—not the
earth, not the sky, not the people, only the poems were
real and the pain. I was lonely. No one understood me
or my kind. No one understood Kentucky. I waited until
my roommate was out to call home. A dark-haired
Southern California beauty she loved to hear me speak
Kentucky. She loved to tell me how she was a dark child
in a family of blondes and had been called nigger as a
child. I learned to keep all that I loved about Kentucky
secret. In the all-white dormitory, when they wanted to
know where I was from, and I would say Kentucky, folks
would laugh and say Where's that. I wanted to move off
campus—to move away. No one told me about the black

dorm on the other side of campus. I was content where I was once I had a room of my own and I stayed there.

She was so innocent then. It was easy to see why they had not wanted her to leave home—to go so far away. There was so much she did not know. Ignorance did not stop her though. When she did not know she asked questions. Her ignorance is a lack she makes up for by having courage as strong and sweet as the best tobacco. When she needed to she fought back. She read poems.

When I first hear about "him" I hear he is a man of words—another poet. An older white woman in my poetry-writing class stares at me. We call each other by our last names. She is Angel. Her skin reminds me of wet white sheets hanging on a line to dry in winter—frozen sheets slightly thawing, the creases like those in her flesh. Her skin is worn and strong and has its own weathered beauty. Her skin attracts me—its stark whiteness caught under dark raven-colored hair. She is finding herself late—after a long marriage—after children. She is finding herself—sometimes alone and always searching. We had something in common. We were both looking to words— to desire. We meet after class to talk—to share the longing in ourselves—the desires we cannot seem to express. She tells me about this black male poet she is sure will desire me. Our dark bodies have become the country she longs to possess—a resource for her under-developed dreams. We will constitute her empire—two bodies she will connect and claim.

· · ·

There had only ever been two kinds of white women in my life—the ones whose homes black women cleaned and the missionary kind—the do-gooders. The woman I met in class was a mixture of the two. Fascinated by everything black, by all forbidden things, this was a white woman making up for lost time in her life. Angel talked endlessly about the brilliant young black man, his looks— his regal bearing. He looked not American, she would say, more African but not so much like a person—like a Benin sculpture—that was it. I was not impressed. I had been around white people long enough to know that their ideas about black beauty were different—that they did not seem to understand a thing about how black folks see ourselves. Whenever Angel had that seductive sound in her voice and that dreamy look in her eyes when she talked about his beauty, I just paused inside and watched with amazement that white folks who understood nothing about us were so sure they knew everything—all our secrets even the secrets of our desires. They don't know us and never will.

6

There is nothing about white folks she wants to know. They have been tried in the courts of black folks' justice and found guilty as charged. They have been found guilty because the blood of the slaughtered is still on their hands. It covers the land, spreads across the nation. Everywhere they call home is a place where blood was shed in their name, in the name of their longing to have a country where they could be free. Everything about their lives is stained with blood. She is afraid of blood. As a child whenever they came close to her she would run or scream. She would hide. She would not speak.

They were in my mind the color of unspeakable things. The pain of someone raped in the night and having to bear in the light of day a history they could never call their own. They were willing to slaughter for things that

45

could be shared, bought, traded. They preferred blood. They were vampires, living off the blood of the slaughtered. It was impossible to touch them without blood leaving its sticky trace. I lived in a world where we kept out distance from white folks. It was our way of not having to bear witness.

I grew up in a state that had an Indian name—Kentucky. I loved the sound of that word, the way it fell off our thick backwoods tongue. It means bloody ground. The blood of Indians mingles with the blood of slaves here. The ground is full of earth-colored red mud and the weight of history. It is as though the dying still bleed here, still leave a trace. I can never really love anyone white with my whole heart. It is not the fact of whiteness that keeps me from this love, it's the fact of history. I hate the sight of blood. In my dreams, when they appear, the white bodies I could love with my whole heart, they are covered in blood.

Whiteness is on the other side of the tracks. When white bodies cross the tracks, when they enter those dark dense spaces of blackness, it is always and only a warning—a sign of danger. When blackness stretches itself across town, beyond the tracks, it is always and only to serve—a sign of submission. When white bodies see black bodies in their utterly white world they know there is nothing to fear. Even when white folks smile and are nice, she has been told to be suspicious, to look behind those smiles to see if danger resides there. She has been told to inspect all the secret places of the mind where hatred could be lingering, where the will to annihilate could be waiting to strike. She has been told all her life You can take what white folks have to offer but you don't have to love them. *These are the harsh lessons she learns living with the world of racial apartheid. These are the signs of its intimate traumas. White people are suspect. They can never let go the fact of whiteness long enough to love.* You can take what white folks have to offer but you don't have to love them.

I learn to be close but not too close. I make friends with the white girl from across the tracks who drives a sleek long white convertible. We meet in the integrated high school. We cross the tracks of race to look for the secret things hidden behind the taboos. We go in search of hidden treasures. We are looking for ourselves beyond the sign of race. Nature is the only place we can go where race leaves us. We can ride in this car way out. We can let the top down on country roads where there is nobody to see us, riding next to each other laughing and drinking ice cold soda pop. At first I am not sure I want to cross the tracks to make nice with a white girl but the smell of the car seduces me. Its leather seats, the real wood on the dashboard, the shiny metal so clear it's like glass—like a mirror it dares us to move past race to take to the road and find ourselves—find the secret places within where there is no such thing as race. On those country roads, the sun heating the backs of our necks, we find a world where there is no black and white—where we can love one another if we want to, a world where there is nothing to fear. For now it is the car I love not Ann, not the white girl who has everything including pain. The white girl who is different from other girls because she can be. It is not the car she drives or the money she spends that makes her different, it is the pain she confronts in secret—the shame she feels that connects us. When she slashes her wrists they want me to explain, to lay all our secrets out in black and white. They want to separate us. I have the right to remain silent. In this world where black and white cannot love, I refuse to say a word. I will not let them see our pain. Later when her wrists have healed, when clean neat razor blade scars are there to remind us even though we are riding again, moving past fields of tobacco waving to us like outstretched arms ready to hold and embrace, we can examine the pain. We listen to each other's stories, talking loud over the sound of the car radio. Those random gusts of wind that can appear on even the hottest days carry our words as we speak together the pain of not being loved enough, of not being chosen, of not even being able to love one another.

I learn to be close but not too close—learn to choose friends who long to journey to the same places I want to go to, who want to find an end to this thing we call race that divides everything in the world we live in. We want to leave behind our skin—forget about black and white. We want to journey to the heart of the matter. Born and bred in the arms of Jim Crow, in the backyard of the Ku Klux Klan, shrouded in the shade of the Confederate flag, we knew everything there was to fear about crossing boundaries. We crossed the tracks in the name of freedom but we were still afraid to love.

He was my best male buddy, my ace boon coon, a lanky funny-looking white buddy with a crooked mouth who always carried a camera in his hand. It was the old slate gray Volvo he drove that brought us together. I had a thing for cars, for riding in cars. I had no desire to drive. The three of us—me, him, and Ann—dreamed of changing the world, of not accepting the boundaries of black and white. Together we defy our parents for friendship. We cross the tracks in the name of a love we cannot know. We believe that the absence of romance between us is not about the barrier of race—that the heart too has its boundaries—that the journey of desire cannot be charted by political longings. We accept the intimacy of friendship while we wait for the world to change. It shelters and sustains us. The three of us share a driving passion, a longing to go to the heart of the matter in the car of our dreams.

Leaving home and going to college no one understands the distances separating the Jim Crow world of her apartheid history and the world the sixties ushered in. She went to college caught between those two worlds— trapped by the boundaries of the divided south and the open spaces of the California frontier. No one understood

49

the trauma of those distances. Everyone in California acted as if race did not matter. It was hard for her. She was always looking past the fiction of racial manners and seeing the nightmare of race lurking in the shadows. Her new life was in an all-white world. The black people who surrounded her were different. The way they stayed together had nothing to do with danger and protection. It was not rooted in understanding the history of blood and pain. They had no relation to the earth. She could not see herself in their eyes. To them she was invisible, a country girl from the south, with old-fashioned religion and a feudal sense of honor, things that had no place in their world. They were the cream of the crop, E. Franklin Frazier's black bourgeoisie. They had traveled the world. They were the children of black diplomats, black professionals. They had no use for the black poor. They despised the south without ever having been there. She went straight to the heart of the matter. Shared race did not mean shared intimacy. She was often alone.

7

These stories are not mine. They are the way I remember
his stories. Hence they do not document; they only inter-
pret. We do not see white folks in the same way. He has
no sense of Jim Crow. Racial apartheid is for him a term
that is just too strong. He has never had to think about
the Ku Klux Klan. To him white people are just like
everybody else—maybe better. He does not even question whiteness. It is not about white people. It is about
the better things in life, culture, education, enlighten-
ment. He does not aspire to be white. He longs for access
and acceptance. If they accept him he must be as good as
they are—better than other black people, better than
most white people. He attends schools with gifted pro-
grams. Always the only exceptional *one* black person, he
learns to enjoy being the object of a desiring white gaze.
He lives in neighborhoods that are white and Mexican

and black people are part of the mix. He does not feel the pain of Jim Crow. Shared black skin does not draw them closer. Her kinda blackness is strange to him. His kinda blackness I have heard about but find it hard to believe. He has traveled. I have not. He has moved—migrated. He understands the difference a region can make. He believes he can love wherever his heart wills. He can love white people as himself.

These different understandings of whiteness separate them. She sees the politics of race in the everyday. Race politics for him are a matter of ideas. He sees race as a fact of life to forget, to move past. His understanding of the heart of the matter is different from hers. The ways she finds whiteness suspect annoy him. He would rather not think about it. He has no desire to go searching in the shadows of anyone's mind to see the dangers lurking within. His world is peopled with white friends, and white lovers. He does not suspect his own need to be the only black person in a sea of whiteness.

I dread meeting his friends. They are the kind of white people I have spent a lifetime wanting never to be in close contact with the kind that have blood on their hands. *They are not renegade white folks like the few friends she had in high school. They are regular old white bread through and through. They are into success, material comfort, into education and culture, but they try not to think too hard about anything. Shocked that he has chosen to have a black girlfriend, they rave about the ex-girlfriend, the whiteness of her skin, her long black hair. The ways they evaluate her, a black female, or hold her in contempt mean nothing. Seeing them, searching the crevices of their minds, she learns about him—learns the ways that they are separate.*

He was not sure when he started to question why his girl-friends were always white. A sexual adventurer, he was eager to be sexual with as many willing partners as possible. Race was not an issue. He was however extremely shy and wary of rejection. White girls just seemed more open, more willing than black girls, less afraid of sex. White girls had no problems with abortions. Black girls attracted him but they always seemed reserved. They always wanted the sex to be a prelude to something else, something he was not ready to give.

Picture this. Little black boys playing in a park. They see a young white girl. To them she is different, strange, exotic. They want to stare at her like she is an animal in a zoo. They want to make their bodies a cage. Capturing her they can look as long as they like. They have no desire to touch. She sees them watching her. Their loud voices ring in her ears like the sound of elephants clamoring through the jungle on Tarzan. She is so sure that they are animals—that they want to tear her to pieces bit by bit and eat her. She cannot see that they are small boys poking fun. White grown-ups bring police. They are taken to a local station. Grown white men threaten to lock them up, tell them they are just animals, that they will end up in a cage.

Raised without fathers these little black boys are driven back into the shadows by fear. Fear is a womb they hide in. The white man's voice is the sound that brings them out of the shadows into the light of scrutiny. The images of the men they will become are sketched by the white man who is all-knowing, a prophet, a god who can protect his children. The white man lays out a genealogy of possibility within which there is no hope. Against this backdrop, this vision of life in a cage, one little black boy begins to dream his future in defiance of the all-knowing white father's words. He will live his life building a mansion but always in front of the cage. The cage is witness. He finds comfort in the white man's gaze, in the fear and surprise in the little white girl's eyes. No longer a spiritual orphan he finds his family and a way to chart his journey home.

We can't agree on whiteness. I always stand at a distance. The gaze of white folks disturbs me. It is always for me the would-be-colonizing look. I hate being the smart black person in the cage. If I had money for all the times some white person wants to know how I made it out of the jungle, I'd be rich. Or if only I were paid for all the times they look at me wondering how I can still be such a primitive, so without manners. I speak my mind, tell the truth. It's country to them. My Kentucky origins explain it all. I have not had the full benefit of their civilization but when I acquire it they are confident I will change. Every white person he brings into our life enters like a missionary. He does not seem to notice. Something in him is affirmed by the way they select him from among those black people who are the exception.

When we first met black militancy had changed the nature of black male desire. It had sanctioned black males turning away from the white female gaze and bonding with sisters. The incestuous nature of the construction said it all. This turning then was really a perversion of desire. The repression of longing for the other in order to choose from one's own kind. When black political leaders dogged the brother with a white girl on his arm or in his bed, he had been unmoved. But when his symbolic black intellectual writer/father Amiri Baraka publicly shifted the nature of his desire, leaving the white woman and her children behind, he was suddenly willing to see those uptight sexually reserved wanting something else black girls in a new way. After all white pussy was just becoming boring, too easy to get, too much of the same thing. It just seemed like everywhere he went, with the exception of the men's room, there was some white girl trying to enter the jungle by pulling down his pants. In the early years of our life together I was constantly reminded of all that he had given up to choose me, his little sister, his woman child. He was attracted to that innocence I brought with me, the experience of never having been alone a day in my life, the experience of having been with only two men sexually, the experience of him being the only one who satisfied. And he liked that underneath that innocence, that cool Snow White like veneer of purity, there was an enflamed heart. Awakening that heat and possessing it was the joy of his life. I thought he liked me because I was so smart, because I read books every day, because I wrote poetry, because I wanted to be a writer. I thought he liked my looks too, that crazy mane of hair that floated around my head like bales of cotton so soft to the touch, so curly when wet, and then so straight when combed out. He liked my body, every bit of it, even as he remembered always that it was not the white body of his repressed longing. It was as though he had entered my body through the space in his mind that was so identified with whiteness that he was coming to black female flesh through the same split between virgin and whore that gave white women everything except the lure of being off limits, taboo. Those smart schoolteacherlike black women with their Egyptian bellies and their tight pussies and their high butts they were off limits to whiteness. Having them one had what the white man could only long for, it was all about perversion.

8

*Sexuality and reading are intimately linked in her mind.
She feels the first stirring of desire when she reads the
books her father hides behind the bed. Desperate for
something to read, something to take to the edge of daily
life, she wanders from room to room of their large two-
story wood-frame house to see if there are any books she
has missed. His hidden books are not to be touched, she
knows that but desperation leads her to overcome her
fear. The word pornography means nothing to her. There
is nothing spoken about sexuality in their house. Everyone believes the pleasures of sexuality must be submerged
under a narrative of sexual horror. Understanding the
horror is what they believe will keep young girls safe—
free of unwanted pregnancy. Sex as she can piece it
together from the endless tales of how horrible it would
be to be homeless and pregnant (since her mama made it*

clear that none of her girls would be bringing any babies into her house) is mainly a thing men want, something that gives men pleasure. From everything they say, it is clear it can only bring women pain that will never go away.

When she discovers his books with names like Passion Pit *and* Love Slave, *she finds a way to sexual pleasure. In her tiny dark room that once belonged to her brother, she can lie in the bed and feel the wetness between her thighs as she reads all about women who long for sex, who beg for it. She longs to be one of those women. And so she reads and reads, until she is caught red-handed, hands between her legs, books under pillow. They say nothing. Her father just stops bringing those books home. Now that they know her secret, she is all the more an outsider in this household of women who want sex to be only for men, something a woman gives in exchange for something else.*

Words awe her. She cannot believe their power— spoken words, written words. In her life there is always a contest between words on the page read silently and the power of words spoken, performed. Her decision to be a poet was the perfect blending of both. She recited poems to her family. She announced to them her true vocation— to write, and write, and never stop writing.

I am always performing words. Maybe it's from being told since very little that I am too dramatic. It's drama they push me toward, performing in this or that play, reciting poems at this or that school function. My fear of performing is overcome by the small space of doing something right that it gives me. In my childhood I was always the one who was yelled at, smacked around, punished for not being able to get it right. Words are something I can get right and I love them.

Her love of words is a private passion—one she would rather not share. In the house of her childhood though everything had to be shared. If she tried to hold anything back, they would search and find the hidden places. Her written words, discovered, read were just the source of more pain and punishment. This was why she loved poetry. They did not always understand it so they left it alone.

I write in secret. Have no interest in sharing my words. It's hard for me to take a creative writing class because I have to share those words with others. Their words have little meaning for me. We live in different worlds. That is what I think throughout my undergraduate years at Leland Stanford University—that my world of Kentucky hills and backwoods has no place here—that it will never be understood.

She does not know how much she intrigues everyone because they see her as somehow primitive, always more naked and raw than everybody. They do not have a clue how common her ways are in the world she comes from and she does not try to give that world to them. Not even when they want her to be a specimen, ethnographic subject, exotica southern belle, black bird from a strange and faraway place.

Everyone makes fun of the south at Stanford; especially Kentucky. It angers and bores me. I content myself with the knowledge that they know nothing about my world. Not even the black folks; they don't have the same ways or speak the same language. They are as foreign to me as the white folks I meet here and often more unaccepting. Neither group moves me. I am so desperately seeking to understand who I am. I cannot belong to any group. My family is the group I am fleeing to find myself. I make a pact the day I leave—no more life in groups.

Mostly she is alone. And if she is in a group you might say she is always performing. That's the only way she can bear the hemmed-in feeling she gets in groups, to be there and not there. This aloneness is sweet to her even as she fears it. Emily Dickinson, her poet friend, long dead but always understanding of her need to think and write alone. Emily Dickinson guides me.

In writing class we have to talk about who influences us and why. I speak passionately about the need to read poetry, to read the works of other poets old and new. I talk about Emily Dickinson. I share without sharing too much. When we leave class it is clear I have a passion for words—that much is shared. I will write poetry all my days and it will not matter what anyone says about the nature of my words.

He has been writing poetry for a long time and knows more. He tells her who to read of the contemporary poets. She is mainly a reader of words no one talks about or reads anymore. Her recitations of Gerard Manley Hopkins, words that were meant to be touched and caressed by the human voice, made no impression on him. He was reading Pound, Eliot, Olson, William Carlos Williams, Robert Duncan, and of course Baraka. He had little use for Adrienne Rich, Langston Hughes, and Wallace Stevens. From him she learned about worlds of poetry, different schools.

We were excited by words together. Poetry had brought us together. It was a true and perfect union. We could lie together after hours of passionate lovemaking and recite poems. This was my dream to be with someone who understood the words, who loved poetry. For the first time in my life I felt understood. There was no need for secrets. Even though I did not like to read my work, we celebrated the necessity of working. I was always quoting biblical poetics to him (he was rarely interested in the bible) but I liked to recite *work while it is day for the night cometh when no man can work*. Writing was our shared passion and around it and with it we were hoping to make a life—a life with poetry at the center—a life with no limits.

9

Perhaps it was the memory of her father saying the word slut—slurring it just so—that made it sound disgusting and evil at the same time. It was the word he used when talking about the way they dressed. He didn't want any daughter of his going out into the world looking like a slut. Sluts were worse than whores—a slut was somebody who had a choice, somebody who could have kept herself from falling but who wanted to fall. Sluts made choices. They were not victims. You could pity a whore but a slut you only despise.

Whenever he said the word slut, I thought he was talking about me. I thought it was something that I had, something about the way I looked. I had something men wanted, something that made me desirable. And that something was dangerous. I hated it when he said the word slut. It was one of the times his hatred of women slipped out, his contempt for them. It was the contempt he held toward all things weak and out of control. Sluts seduced men, made them turn away from their good churchgoing women, from their good lives, turn away craving female flesh in a way that made them weak. A man chasing after a slut was a weak thing in his eyes. I knew that even then. Slut was not a word he used often. He saved it for the bad times, saved it for the times when they might have been overly excited about getting dressed up and going somewhere special. Just his saying the word slut could put them in their place, close down their desire as though a door had been slammed shut.

It was more common to hear him go on and on about backstreet women. Somehow he made them believe that any female no matter how young or old with the potential to be a slut was destined to live as a backstreet woman. She would never be any man's wife—the person he would choose to take home, the person that would be taken to meet family.

I was afraid that I would be nothing but a backstreet woman. Daddy had handed us that fear. Only I more so than my sisters seemed to have taken it on, found myself in nightmares living in shadows, finding my way down dark alleyways, trapped—a backstreet woman. It was that fear that made me want to rush into living with him so soon. I was too smart—too sassy. Those were the ways of backstreet women. Sassy to seduce, smart to take all a man got without giving all you got in return. Somehow

I knew, even then as a girl, that backstreet women kept something for themselves. They were not like wives who gave it all away in return for not being held in contempt.

She had not been able to understand, then, in her girl-hood why being smart with books and words was dangerous, but she knew that it was making her into something no man would want as a wife. She was not even surprised when the high school drama teacher, a skinny white woman with reed-thin lips, had told her she would never find a husband, at least not any black man. You are, she had told her, too smart for any black man to love. In her drama classes she had felt a freedom never experienced anywhere, a freedom that defied the confine-ment of home, of her father's world. And yet there she was getting the same message about the danger of being too smart, too full of words, and how being smart might make you become something men might desire but never something in his right mind any man could love. These messages frightened and hurt. And she was determined not to take them to heart.

I took them to heart though. My way of taking them to heart was to believe that I could make it not so. I could find me a man to love me. And I did. And when I found him he told me the only woman to desire was a smart woman, a woman who could keep your mind working and your dick hard. He told me that the only women who were really open to life were smart women. They had open mouths and wet pussies. They were not afraid to desire. I had chosen well—someone who loved me for my mind and my body too.

She thought he loved her for her mind. He was enchanted with her smart talk, her blunt speech, her ways of thinking about the world. Yet still and all he did not take her seriously. She did not know that though—not then, not in the beginning.

He acted as though it was only natural that I was smart, not anything strange or unusual. He made me feel as though it was only natural that I wanted to be a writer. He was the same as me or so it seemed. With him the part of me that longed to think and think found a place. I was no longer in hiding. I was able to open my mouth and say everything I was thinking with no fear of being punished, no backhand lick, no confinement in a dark airless space, no bruises and welts to remind me that I should be seen and not heard. Finally, I believed childhood was over and with it the pain and the shame.

She is blind to how he really sees her because she is arrogant—not in a bad way. You might say it's the arrogance of innocence. Like that wild child they found in the woods once and tried to bring into civilization, who had his own ways that he would cling to with all his might. She has her ways. Her courage and will excite him. But for how long. How long will he be enchanted. How long before the spell breaks.

.　.　.

In my father's eyes, I am really a backstreet woman, living in sin, living with a man I am not married to. Just because I am educated and in college *that don't change nuthin.* That's what mama reports when I say I am living with him. She pleads with me to think about marriage, now before it's too late. Mama seems to have forgotten that fateful day when I declared I will never marry. I can still see myself, schoolbooks in hand, sweater dangling from one arm, walking up those stairs to the atticlike rooms I shared with her and my sisters. There is a point you reach on the stairs where you can look down and still see somebody at the bottom. It was at that crucial point in my sixteenth year that I turned and said to mama with a conviction that startled me, I will never marry. I will never belong to any man. I was courageous and defiant then.

But it wasn't courage or defiance that made her want to live with him after only a few months of dating. It was the fear of being used and left behind, of being a backstreet woman. He kept saying he did not want to move in with her too soon. Yet when she arrived in the night one day with most of her belongings, he just accepted his fate. Vaguely, he remembered agreeing that it was fine. Still he held it against her that she moved in because she wanted to even though he had doubts, even though he was not ready.

66

10

Love left her. She could not remember the how and why of it only the feeling of being loved and then having love go away. She could vaguely recall the feeling of being loved only it was the anguish of abandonment that most stayed with her. She was not even clear who the anguish belonged to only that it lingered. It was the knife in her heart no one could pull out. It was the blood flowing from body into death no one could see. No she did not love. All those times when she was claiming to love, she was really seeking to escape the anguish of unforgotten abandonment. She did not fall in love with him. She was drowning. She needed him to save her life. He was her rescue and her sanctuary. She believed it was love. She had to. She was loyal—a woman of her word. It was a matter of honor.

When it was time to tell him I loved him—when it was what every romance had determined I should do—I spoke in the name of will. I will love. Love as an action not a feeling only. I will love. In the early days of having sex with him (when he could see me, when the Gypsy woman would leave now and then on her own small journeys) I would make love as though my body existed only as the fulfillment of his desire. It was an instrument— surrendered to the feeling of sexual ecstasy. With him I discovered my flesh. In no way physical in other locations of life, I suddenly found my body exerting force and power through longing. Sex was sweet communion. It was my body. Sometimes in the midst of all-consuming desire I could hear the words from communion *Take, eat, this is my body*. I could hear Gary Snyder reading the words from a poem *is this our body*. It was a poem about seeing nakedness for the first time and being renewed.

In sex I felt as though the body that had died too long ago, somewhere in my girlhood, was resurrected. I was living again fully and deeply. I began to eat. Up until then, eating was always boring, a task I forgot or could not get back to. Passion made me hungry. And I began to eat and eat. I was not a slave of love. I was enslaved by passion. But I called it love—that was the only word powerful enough to make him think of leaving her to be with me. And then it was his declared love that hesitated. Maybe he was ready to let her go—but he was not sure about rushing into anything with me. I pushed and pressured. I wanted him to declare his love in action—to live with me—to make a life.

·　·　·

*In girlhood, she was convinced that her longing to be a
writer and a thinker would always stand in the way of
love. It was what her parents told her. Their words were
echoed in schools by thin white teachers with stringy
dyed blond hair who made her their "pet" even as they
explained in hushed tones that black men would not
desire her because she was just too smart. Of course since
any meangingful desire between a black woman and a
white man was unthinkable—unheard of, always and
only rape, an act of degradation and humiliation or so the
south had taught them and taught them well—to say
no black man would desire her was to hold only the
choice of being smart and being alone. She was determined. This would never be her destiny. It was that deter-
mination to not be seduced and abandoned that made her
pressure him. In their many talks about living together
he finally agreed even though he was unclear about
the time.*

I knew he was unclear. I however had made up my mind.
I came to his house one day with my belongings all
packed into a friend's tiny car. He expressed amazement
that I had acted so quickly when we had just reached an
agreement. I pushed aside his hesitation wanting to know
why did it matter now or later if it was what we both
wanted. He had three black cats then. They belonged to
the Gypsy woman. She had just left them. I wanted to

69

send them to her along with the clothes she left behind—
clothes I loved to wear.

*In keeping with her attitudes about free love, she had
never questioned the rights of the Gypsy woman. She
had never questioned his love for her. In her mind it was
possible to love more than one person. Naturally then,
when this mysterious woman called and wanted to meet
with her, she did not hesitate. When she spoke of this
impending meeting to friends they were quick to say that
she was making a mistake. One should never meet the
other woman. She disagreed. Being feminist, she believed
that in patriarchy men—all men—were trained from day
one to lie (whether they chose to was a different issue).
Growing up every grown woman understood this—men
lie. The difference was that those women blamed it on
nature. She saw it always as a choice. It was always an
issue of allegiance, whether to be loyal to women or other
men. Men lie to make male domination work better. It
was that simple. Nothing so complex as nature.*

Even though I had always been taught that men lie to
women—that it is their nature—he was not like other
men. So naturally when she called me that day and
demanded to know who I was and what I was doing in
her life—in her relationship—telling me that she knew
nothing about them having an open relationship, I was
deeply disappointed. Naturally when she wanted to see
me, I could not turn her away. After all I had been
changing the nature of her relationship. I was an accom-

70

plice in acts of betrayal. And I felt stupid and just a bit ashamed that I had been so willing to believe him— that it had not occurred to me to call her and confirm the truth of his words. The day she came was gray and wet. She looked tired and beat. I had made my favorite foods. She did not want to eat with me. She wanted to talk, really to ask me to leave her man be. At that moment I was more concerned with the fact that he had lied. I wanted to make sense of it. I shared with her my thoughts about jealousy—that it was all a waste, that none of us could really keep anyone where they don't want to be. And even if they choose to be a prisoner of our love, it never really satisfies. She seemed not to know what to say. When it was time to go she merely insisted that he loved her. I simply said I hope he loves you—I could not respect a man who would live for so many years with a woman he did not love. We walked together in the rain to her bus stop. I never saw her again. I stopped wearing her clothes. The only piece of her that stayed behind was a book of recipes written in longhand. I learned to cook using those recipes. He loved her cooking.

The Gypsy woman had no idea what she would encounter coming to meet me. It was no doubt hard for her to arouse the necessary outrage and hostility toward this small southern childlike black woman. Like every white woman with a black man, she had always imagined this moment, when his real desire for a black woman would surface and he would leave her. She did not have black women friends. She did not even know what they were like. It was precisely this space of unknowing that had been the breeding ground for fear. It was not just that this new woman was black but also that she was younger—years younger. Together the two things defeated her. She knew then it was over and done with—their life together—that it was that simple.

Naturally, mama did not approve. I told her everything. She thought I was coldhearted. She said to me If he will leave her that way he will leave you that way too. I did not doubt the truth of her words. I only thought then that if the time has come for him to go then nothing will keep him. I reminded her that men leave women all the time—in the same way—even if there is no other woman. I tell her: I thought you taught me, Men will leave—it's their nature. Mama was wiser than me. She knew that I did not really believe he would leave me—ever. I wanted to live with him forever. That was the way we did it back home.

She did not want to marry. She told her mother that nineteen was too young for marriage, that the soul still had so much growing to do that when she looked into her future it was not marriage she saw. She did not tell her mother or him that she feared marriage would bind her to him forever. She did not want to be bound. She wanted to stay of her own free will—for love. She had decided to love him. And she did—in her own way.

Our life was centered on two desires—the longing to write and the longing to live in a constant state of sexual

72

bliss. When we were not fucking we were busy writing. He has his writing space and I have mine. I hate to work in the same room with somebody else. It is too easy for me to notice them and forget myself. I am used to being alone. I need to be private always. He respects this longing for privacy. It is me who stands provocatively at the door of his study luring him away from words.

She learns about sex from him. To make her laugh, he quotes long passages from the Marquis de Sade. He teaches her that women really have the power in sex with men, that it is the man who is vulnerable and afraid. She has had too little experience. She believes he knows better. She believes because there is no feeling of vulnerability in her passion. She is not afraid to let go—to surrender. She trusts him when he speaks about sexuality. They will not fight about the body. They will fight about words.

In the beginning I thought that being with him would help me to be a better writer. And it did help—in the beginning. He was older than me, seven years older, and was much more confident. He had attended an Ivy League school. While we were both from working-class backgrounds, he had taken on different class values. Groomed throughout high school to excel in a white world, he had always known where he was headed—that he would work toward a Ph.D., be a professor, write. I knew I wanted to write. I did not think about having a career, good schools versus bad schools. The Ivy League meant nothing to me. I had difficulty with school, with the way we were taught. He was comfortable with the process.

During the first months of living together we took the same class in medieval literature. Though we frequently copied each other's homework, he always received a higher grade. The white-haired male professor always treated me as though I was stupid. As a quiet intellectual black male he always received approval from academic white folks. Not one to challenge the system, he was more accepted. And of course he had attended the right schools.

Early on then in our love life we confronted differences in how the world would respond to us, especially white folks. All too often folks chose one of us to label good and the other bad. Having been involved in relationships with white partners we could both see the difference it made when we were two bright black folks together. Suddenly, we were looked at with suspicion. As though it was the oddest thing in the world for two bright aspiring gifted black folks to be passionately interested in one another. It was evident to us that our bonding was seen as political—some aberrant admiration of blackness in a world where so many folks just assumed that the goal of our lives was to assimilate into the white mainstream as smoothly and as swiftly as possible. Having white partners was one way to make that transition.

We were happy to be together. Our shared blackness mattered. It always mattered more to me than to him. A black world was familiar to me. I saw nothing unusual

74

about a black woman and man together. He was not as comfortable with blackness. It was in the white world that he experienced himself as special, that he felt his intelligence most affirmed. The world of whiteness was for him a place to escape some of the harsh realities of being young, gifted, and black.

Blackness was most real for him in the world of music and poetry. He was into black music. When I first met him he worked as a DJ. On Friday nights we would drive the long distance to the station and I would sit and read while he played jazz and music from around the world. His voice was different. Coming over the airwaves it sounded husky and deep, the way gravel sounds when a car drives over it on a still night. I liked his radio voice. I never .liked listening to music while reading. This was something he could never understand. In his world music made everything better—even reading.

We were officially in love. That meant slowly sharing friends with one another. I had very few friends. My ex-roommate and closest friend Carolyn did not care for him. To her he was cold and aloof—not warm like me. Since we had never believed in the attraction of opposites she expressed fear. He made her feel afraid. I brushed her fear away. She was not afraid of that innocent-looking blond-haired male who left bruises on her white skin. Mack had no look of innocence. I did not see him as cold. He just seemed quiet and still. Stillness in a man was attractive to me.

When she took him home for the first time, she was amazed at her sisters' reactions. They kept saying He's so much like daddy and you always hated daddy growing up. She could not remember always hating daddy. She could not remember loving him much either. To her he was just cold and distant. She did not see him as being quiet and still. Daddy was cold and distant, a hard and angry manner. Mack was not like daddy. She just could not see how they could think it.

Her parents did not believe in free love. They were not allowed to sleep in sin at her parents' house. It was bad enough that she was already setting a bad example for her sisters by living with a man and not being married, bad enough that she had brought him home—but to have sex with him under their roof, that would have been too bold. They would never have let her forget. She would be forever seen as violated and violating. He had no interest in being in her parents' house. He wanted to have sex.

I could not imagine having sex with any man in my parents' house. In their house in some way I am always a child. He wanted to do it there, to defy them. I did not understand this desire. One night we stayed awake while everyone else was sleeping, kissing and touching each other with our clothes on. It reminded me of high school, of crazed longings when boys would come over and one of my sisters would be sent to stand guard—to watch so that nothing sexual would happen. This memory excited me. I unzipped his pants there on my knees in the darkness of my parents' house and sucked his dick until he came in my mouth. Pleasure and danger were there in that passion—the memory of boys afraid to come to our house cause Mr. Veodis might kill them. They all knew Mr. Veodis didn't let nobody mess with his girls. Down on my knees in the dark house of my childhood I was no longer Mr. Veodis's girl, I was my own woman, taking desire into my own hands. There were no spies in the house of love that night. It was our ritual marriage. I had broken the allegiance of family to be loyal to him. Love and betrayal were linked then.

In the dark loneliness of my bed that night, I dreamed that the spies had found me there down on my knees, that I could hear mama's voice threatening, telling me to wait till your daddy comes home. In the dream I am still on my knees when he arrives, carrying the little black strap from Baba's house. I wondered in my dream why she would have given him her strap. He lashes out at me, screaming. The black leather cut my flesh. I awakened from this dream, my face wet, mama standing near the bed wanting to know what was wrong. Like old times my tears had awakened her. Like old times in the distance I could hear her voice like warm honey telling me to go back to sleep. There was no talk between us about love. Mama had forgotten love. Desire only made her feel afraid.

11

Family is everything. That was the way she had been raised in the clan of her grandmother. Her father's people had always been in the background. The world of her mother had shaped her sense of family and kin. When she was little, folks used to say that her people came from the backwoods with all that shooting and cussing and fighting they did—that was the telltale sign of not being city bred, of being from the country or the hills.

When I was a girl, Baba my mama's mother taught me about family—taught me that family was everything. Within the family it was important to keep one's word—to tell the truth. Your word was your bond Baba would say. I did not understand the meaning of the word bond, but I looked it up in the big grown folks' dictionary and found it meant that which binds or holds together. It enchanted me to imagine our family held together by the strength of our word. Then there were the endless lessons about loyalty. To choose a friend over family was to invite punishment. One had to be loyal to family first and then to friends. Words like honor and loyalty were crucial to my understanding of kin. To know anyone and what they were worth one had to know their people.

They—mama, her sisters and brothers—always spoke of Baba's world as "over home." No doubt to distinguish it from the home they had made as grown women and men who had left the house of their father. It was still the primary meeting place. Her aunts and uncles rarely came to each other's homes. They met at Baba's. There everything was discussed, fought about, there the cussing and fighting took place. Her mother Rosa Bell could not stand to be there in the midst of all the loud talk but loyalty meant one had to go. All the commitment to loyalty and honor had its downside. When anyone believed that family honor had been called into question it was necessary to defend the clan or its individual members. One could kill and die for honor—one could kill and die in the name of that word that was the bond.

When I first took him home, my folks were surprised that I knew so little about his people. To not know was in violation of family codes. I had tried to talk to him about family but his was broken and scattered in ways that made it difficult for him to speak of them and hard for me to understand when he did speak. It was one of those subjects we left hanging—that we kept intending to get back to but never did. He grew up living with his mother, a solitary child. His older brothers and one sister had been raised more by their grandmother on their mama's side. He was just not that into family. I could not accept that. To not know his family was to not know him. I demanded to meet his mother.

She was too young then, too innocent, unable to see the danger when he did not want her to meet his mother. Like so many other things he cared for, he wanted his mother all to himself. She did not know it then but she was competition. She could be embraced by his mother in a way that no white woman ever could, no matter how much his mother might care for any white female he would choose to bring home. She could not know that he was worried that this relationship with her might bring him closer to home than he ever wanted to be. And he, even though he wanted to possess home, wanted to know that he could own it if he wanted to, he did not want to go home again. She on the other hand could not imagine life without home.

I want to meet his mother. His daddy was dead. Mystery surrounded him. Mack had never really known his father who was from Panama. Old pictures of him revealed the lovely self-satisfied smile of an immigrant in a new land finding hope and the promise of a better future. They lived in Florida then. Drinking turned that life of hope into another dead end. He was just a little boy and had few memories of that time. One day his mother decided to leave, to follow her mother who had decided to come west with the white folks she worked for. This part of his story fascinated me. I had never heard of any black folks leaving their family to follow white folks. His grandmother, like mine, held the power in their family. Her children followed her west, had their own children, and their lives took root there in sunny Southern California.

It was my first time coming to Southern California. I was anxious. The day before we were to leave I went to a beauty parlor in east Palo Alto to get my hair done. I just wanted a wash and a cut. The hairdresser convinced me though that I would look so much better with a little relaxer in my hair. Since I was a little girl, black beauty parlors have been a place of mystery and longing for me. Growing up I always had my hair done at home. Grown women, and folks with extra money, sent their children to the beauty parlor. It was a place I wanted to go. Like any magical world, when I entered it, I felt as though I relinquished all rights in my body. Just like Alice in Wonderland falling down the hole with no control over what happens, the beauty parlor was a space where I had no control. That day in east Palo Alto when the hairdresser was done with me, I had Barbie doll hair—as straight and as dead as any corpse's.

It was a hairdo my mama would have loved. I was devastated. Here I was going home to meet his mother looking like someone other than myself. When I came home, he yelled and screamed wanting to know what I had done to myself. He made it seem that somehow this hairdo could not be seen by his mother—that she would just not understand. I washed and washed and washed my hair to get the relaxer out—to try and make myself over. I went back to the beauty parlor so that the hairdresser could cut most of it away and my natural hair could grow back.

All my life I have been told by black folks that I am so lucky to have good hair. Yet I hated my hair. It wasn't straight enough to be straight. It wasn't nappy enough to be nappy. It was this in between kinda hair that had no appeal. I wanted thick nappy hair that could be done in all kinda styles. Hair like my older sister Theresa had. Hair had always been my issue. Growing up my sisters loved to play with my hair. It was the next best thing to doll's hair. They combed, plaited, styled. I sat still as any mannequin while they worked on me doing what they wanted to do. Maybe it was this same stillness that paralyzed me when I entered the beauty parlor—that left me with no strength or will to determine my hair destiny.

She was so naive. She couldn't see that he really did not want to take her home, that the hair represented for him a way out. She couldn't see even that he was sending her the message that she on the inside of herself was not good enough to go home and meet his family. A black girl was not a prize to this family that had come from the south to the west following the white folks they worked for. She could not see that it was his contempt for her, his rage that she had moved into the center of his life, that was expressed when he raged about her hair, when he humili-

ated her. The white girls he had loved had never wanted to go home and meet his mother. He could present them when he was ready. Like trophies presented at the end of a game. They were to be a sign of his success, of his having left the past behind, of his having left blackness. She was not a sign of progress. And her journey over to east Palo Alto—to the black section of town—to get her hair done revealed her retrograde tendencies.

The trip to Southern California like all the other car journeys they would make was full of tension. Closed in the car together they were like two big cats in a small cage at the zoo. On a good day they would be warm and close. On a bad day it was all growling and snarling. On a bad day, being locked in together was danger. Since he did not want to take her home, it was a bad day. Everything went wrong. Again she was just too used to being at fault, to being punished, I mean that was her childhood story, to recognize the way he picked at her, the way he used words as though they were sharp little straight pins, which he would stick into her body until she cried out. She did not see him sticking the pins because the way he treated her was so familiar—so much of the fragment of her childhood past, but it was just that, a fragment—different enough that she actually believed that in coming together with him she had managed to escape the pain of the past. It seems so silly now. She did not see that the way he talked her down, with his criticisms and his insistence that she was always a failure, always not quite right, was just a carryover of all that she had endured in *childhood. She had no idea that she had not escaped home cause even when she felt pain there was still happiness. When she thought of home, she could not always remember the happiness.*

The ride to Southern California was too long—too hot. I began to regret wanting to do this. I felt that he was punishing me. Then I thought this was just my craziness. I always thought I was being punished. The problem was that I could not drive—that, as he never stopped telling me, I wanted to make this trip but I had not thought about the fact that he would have to do the driving. I could tell when he did not want to talk with me because he would withdraw into silence, close himself away, like shutting a door, I could not enter. We rode most of the way in silence. I was afraid to say when I needed to use the rest room. He never wanted to stop.

When we arrived in the place where he grew up, it looked lonely and vacant—the way places can look in Southern California—empty like no one lives there. It was so different from the houses I grew up in. There were no apartment buildings in our childhood. Everyone lived in houses and shacks. And the only difference between a house and a shack was that the shack was falling apart and probably could never be mended. His mother lived in a pink adobe apartment building. She kept her blinds closed. When we opened her door, her voice spilled over like sunlight as she embraced her son. At that moment he seemed like an only child, not someone with brothers and a sister. Between him and this woman he called mother there was no room for anyone else. I was an object to be looked over—to be examined with care to see if I was a worthy sign of his being a success. There was no sunlight-filled warm embrace for me. I was the intruder. And I needed more than anything to use the bathroom. On my way there I could see that his mother liked the color pink, that she liked order, that she liked everything to be in its place. It made me uncomfortable that she gave us her big bedroom and slept in the little room. I had not been raised in a world where grown-ups or elders surrendered their beds. I felt shy in this house.

His family took my shyness for weakness. They picked at me too, mostly poking fun at his not wanting to stop during the long ride, at my need to use the bathroom. His aunts joined in the fun. One, the wife of his only and favorite uncle, was impressed by me and bothered at the same time. This aunt lived her life in constant competition with his mother. In his family it was easy to see the ties that bind and harder to see the love. They were close-knit but it was more to do with a network of obligations. It was as though the family was a little minibusiness. Everything was about competition and exchange. Unlike the country people with whom I had been raised, there was no such thing as honor that bound each person to another. I was out of my element but I tried.

I was glad when we left. In keeping with the way I had been raised, I now knew more about him, just like Baba had taught us. Everything I now knew disturbed. One thing was clear: I would never be a daughter in this family. His sister was terribly neglected—unloved for reasons that were frighteningly simple—it was just a world where women were not valued. The grand matriarch core of this family had no use for women. Her interest was always with the power of men. She had cared for her daughters harshly, believing only that the hope of her future rested with her son. She worshiped at the throne of his maleness. He worshiped at the throne of her belief in him. They were the perfect couple. They lived happily next door to one another. He did business with the street, working as a fence. He did legitimate work. Like all the other setters he had come west to make it—to change the winds of fate so that his life would be prosperous and therefore happy. His mother was the explorer who had led the way. She believed in his truths and he believed in hers. This uncle was the closest to a father's care that Mack had known. It was a kind unemotional care. The strength of their bond was rooted in his uncle's power. He could come to the rescue. He could satisfy desire. Living alone in the cozy apartment of his mother, Mack found in his uncle's presence the possibility of adventure. He saw etched on his uncle's face a blueprint of the man he would become, stern, private, never letting anyone into his deepest thoughts, kind when necessary, and able to provide for those closest to him, for those he had chosen.

From what I saw on that first short visit, his relationship with his mother, patterned after the relationship of her mother to her son, had a semblance of mutual devotion without respect. His mother carried too much rage at men to give him the manlove that his grandmother had given her son. Underneath the nods and bows his mother made in the direction of male power was a contempt fierce and deep. She fundamentally did not believe men could be counted on. She was then always on guard, even against her sons. The mother of three sons—the oldest ones she had let go their way. They were mostly raised by her mother. She had chosen Mack—the dark one. The little boy who did not favor his father or his brothers. The little boy who came late in her life—too late to be wanted. She had brought that little boy with her when she came to California leaving her other children behind. They always held it against him—his closeness to her. She had breast-fed him, kept him close to her body longer than she should have. It was her youth and womanliness she was clinging to. The child was just the place for that clinging.

Supposedly, she had left her husband because he was sinking into drink, letting spirits overtake his mind and being. Her drinking was different; she did not lose control. She was a quiet drinker, the kind no one sees as alcoholic in black life. A sign of drinking too much was being out of control, disorderly. To just sit quietly and drink oneself to death was acceptable. It caused nobody pain. Even the first time we visited, though, I could see drink changed her, made her harsh, unleashed the rage and hostility. I tried to imagine what it was like growing up in the solitariness of these changing moods. He learned to shut himself away—to withdraw and retreat. He hid, closing himself away in his room listening to music. That was the raft that kept him from drowning— listening to music. He would sneak records he had bought into the home so she would not unleash rage about money foolishly spent.

Most of his mother's rage at men came out around the issue of money. She worked hard for every red cent. She never let him forget how hard she was working. She wanted him to make up to her for having to work so hard, for having to be the sole provider with no real pleasure in life that did not come from a bottle, a cigarette, and the bright-colored glow they created around a world that was usually dark, murky, and full of too much pain. He, like all the black boys before him living with solitary mothers without grown men to love and care for them, wanted to make it up to her, wanted to give her the world. But the world he gave was never enough. He was always lacking.

If the truth were really told, everyone would know that even though she had always kept him with her, he was not her favorite. He was her necessity, her lifeline. Her favorite was the son named after the father—the one with Junior after his name. Yet this son had abandoned her just like that, without a word. He had become a man, gone into the army, and just left the world of family behind. It was a level of forgetfulness that pained her. Another body she had loved with a sweetness that had become bitter. She kept the younger son with her but she had no sweetness left for him. Every gesture of care was tainted with the bitterness of loss and regret. I had come to know his people and that knowing did not make it easier to love him. It made the hurt in him visible.

She did not know then that he wanted a woman to love him who would never see the hurt.

From the people of the backwoods I have learned that we can see into each other's hearts if we want to; that there is really never any need for words; that if you want to know a person you have to take a good look inside them, to move on inside their flesh, to open the doors of their heart and take a look. From the people of the backwoods I have learned that looking into a body this way can be violating, that it is always necessary to look only to be of service, and not to use what is seen for power. It is the difference between magic that heals and magic that hurts. The therapist wants me to tell him what is in his heart. When I look I turn away and we stop seeing one another.

It was when I met him that this longing to die began to really leave me. By being the mirror into which I could look and see myself with new eyes, he saved me. According to the old ways, the ways of the backwoods, I owed him allegiance always. To be loyal, to keep one's word, to act with integrity. These were the values that I offered him.

He found her values quaint and really quite disturbing. They were to his prep school Ivy League college-educated mind strange and not very useful when it came to living in the modern world. He did admire her courage. And her loyalty was important to him. He found she was faithful. Indeed wasn't she always quoting that verse from the Bible it is required and understood that a man be found faithful. *Of course her notion of being faithful was connected less to deeds than to the spirit informing deeds.*

It's true. I learned from the backwoods people that it was no use trying to possess anyone. I learned from them that wild things need to roam free, that you have to let things go and come. I learn the hurt in life, the anguish jealousy causes. I learn about "free love" in high school when we study utopian movements. I am convinced that women will be safer if we put our faith in free love.

She believed in commitment and constancy. To be true to one's heart was the foundation of everything. She had not learned that from wild spirits but rather from Daddy Gus, her mother's father, her favorite man in the whole world. He loved and adored but most importantly he accepted her just as she was. It was he who told her constantly not to take the pain to heart, but to know that in the end she would have her way and her peace. He was love in her life.

12

My obsession with aesthetics I inherit from Baba, mama's mother. Her house is this incredible place of magic and creativity. A lover of antiques, she always has a story to tell about this piece came from this old white man her mama Bell Blair Hooks worked for. And on and on. I listened to those stories with patience cause Baba was warmest when she was talking about the past. In the present she is a cold woman and often downright mean. Just as she's been married to my grandfather Daddy Gus for more than seventy years, this man she does not sleep in the same bed with, she has lived in this house forever. And with the help of her sons and daughters she has added rooms.

Baba is an artist. Although she cannot read or write, she is a maker of beautiful and exquisite quilts. And much as I want to be like her, even though she teaches me how to piece a quilt, I just can't do it right. Sewing is never going to be my thing. But I long to climb the "stairway to heaven" with her (that's what I call the upstairs in her house—cause it's there that she has her special sewing room). It's a huge room with material everywhere and a sewing machine with a pedal.

Only when she is in a good mood will she take us upstairs and show us her treasures. Mama gets annoyed with us for dragging Baba, old as she is, up those steps. And one day her heart does stop for a bit as she is dragging treasures out of her trunks. Luckily not for me to see. Baba is an eccentric. She is the woman I most want to be like in the world when I am a girl, because she lives like a free spirit flouting convention. That's why she has those chickens and goats and other animals in her backyard even though there is a city ordinance forbidding their presence. And she grows gardens of vegetables and flowers that folks come to see. She believes in the power of beauty to sustain us.

Her love of beautiful things, of making beauty, never seems to warm her heart. She is in her element being stern, dictatorial, and sometimes ruthless. While I will never love her in the way that I love my grandfather Daddy Gus, who cares for the nourishment of my soul, I learn from her how to have the courage to be whoever I must be in the world. Again and again she says the opposite of what mama says. She tells me to remember Play with a puppy he'll lick you in the mouth. She tells me not to give a good goddamn what other folks think cause they can kiss her black ass and take their mammy-made asses back where they came from. Baba cusses all the time. From her I learn to enjoy the power of cursing. She is not afraid to get angry, to yell and fight. Unlike Daddy Gus whom we never hear say a harsh word to anybody.

Baba's tenderness shows through when we roam around the upstairs room, looking at the pictures of her youngest daughter Hattie Lou who died young, after having her second baby. Sometimes she says I look like Hattie, hold my hands in that strange way Hattie used to hold hers. And then we spread out the quilts, my favorite is one made from mama's summer dresses and the dresses of her sisters. There is a story behind each dress, who made it, the occasion they were making it for.

When I leave home I take my quilt with me, even though mama objects. Baba loves the world of the past and has no interest in the new but mama is obsessed with the new. And so she cannot understand my dragging this old thing. But I want it there to cover me, to be my constant reminder of who I am and where I am coming from. I am coming from a long line of fierce and brave country women who know what they need to do in this world and who know how to do it. I always wanted to be more of the kinda girl Baba could have taken to heart and called her own, a girl into making lye soap, wringing the necks of chickens, and sipping newly made wine or drinking large mugs of buttermilk with my corn bread. But she does not read or write and these are my worlds—the worlds I share with Daddy Gus. Baba and I are in the same world

when it comes to telling stories, wanting to surround ourselves with beauty, and believing we can create that
beauty, that there is nothing a woman cannot do that a
man can. Baba teaches me these things. Mama is more
concerned that we know a woman's place. I like it that
Baba sees every place as a woman's place.

When I leave home, I carry with me an understanding of the world I want to create in my home—an aesthetics of existence that will express my needs. Every
room in Baba's huge house is different and every room
has its own story. Later when I read Virginia Woolf's *A
Room of One's Own* I think about my grandmother's
imagination—the world she created for herself and
her own.

A world where she carries on the traditions of the
backwoods and does not care what the neighbors think.
Her next-door neighbor is her sister, Aunt Neely. The
sizes of their houses speak to the differences in their lots
in life. Baba's house is huge and her land stretches, Aunt
Neely has a small house. And even though she keeps it
spotlessly clean and ordered, with only a few precious
objects (dolls she has had forever), she is a drinking
woman. Baba despises strong drink and never touches
the stuff. In her old age drunk with her friends Aunt
Neely dies in a fire that burns down her baby dollhouse.
Baba's house is untouched. No one knows how the fire
started, but it could always be a cigarette left burning.

This is tobacco country and all these women and men
smoke. They roll their cigarettes and smoke like fiends.

And they can't believe any nonsense that says smoke is bad for your health, for they are old and healthy and living well and smoking every minute. They do concern themselves with the evils of alcohol. As Baba says Alcohol ain't been good to this family. There are too many drinkers who can't hold their liquor, whom it will destroy, burn them from the inside out, just like Aunt Neely's house burns with nothing left to remind us of the order and neatness of her being.

Baba's other sister my Aunt Lizzie (short for Elizabeth) also has her house. But hers is the modern one. And she is into modern things like makeup, jewelry, and heavy sweet perfume. Baba wears no makeup and braids her long straight black hair. All these old ladies look white. Tall and elegant, Baba and Aunt Lizzie look like twins but they are as different as night and day. Mama should have been Aunt Lizzie's child. Like her she loves the world of things—of the new. From my aunt Lizzie I will receive a sapphire and gold ring. Her husband my uncle Eliza is the sweetest man in our life next to Daddy Gus. Like Baba and Daddy Gus, Aunt Lizzie and Uncle Eliza have been together forever, even though they sleep in the same bed.

This is the world of women folk I take with me when I leave to college. A world of women choosing and making life as they want to live. I make no connection between their choices and age. They are married and unmarried, some with lots of children and some with none, and they are all women with rooms of their own. Mama thinks this "room of your own" stuff that I bring home form college is nonsense, that Baba, Aunt Lizzie, and Aunt Neely were all women from another time. She thinks I should let that old stuff go. No matter, I am claiming their lives as my birthright and keeping me a room of my own to create and invent and make my world.

Mack does not understand this obsession I have with a room of my own, and even another bedroom if possible, where we don't always have to sleep together. He does not mind working in the same room with someone else, but I need a space that is all mine. That has nothing in it that I have not chosen—a space for precious things. In my space I bring quilts, coils of braided tobacco, the stuff from Kentucky that means nothing to nobody else but me. Everything in my room reminds of who I am and where I am coming from.

At first I long to live in a huge house like Baba's where I can really find my space of solitude. Then the more I think about the planet earth, the more I want to live simply, to occupy as little space as possible. I like finding spaces for us to live with lots of little rooms, so one can escape and yet not be too greedy about space. Mack would like a really big house with huge rooms but he is not interested enough in houses to find us places to live. In all our spaces he has a room that he lives in as he wants to, arranging everything according to his desire. The rest of the house is mine to arrange everything according to the needs of the space and my own longing.

13

Living in a world of racial apartheid where custom and conventions invented to separate black and white lasted long past an end to legal racial discrimination, those who are powerless—black folks—must be overly aware of small details as we go about our lives to be sure we do not enter forbidden territory—to be sure we will not be hurt. You learn to notice things. You learn where not to walk, the stores you don't want to go in, the white people you should not look directly in the face. And you learn to turn away from your own pain and memory and even though you have turned away the memory of past injustice lingers—comes into the present and you cannot live the way other people live.

When I first came to Stanford, it was hard for me because I felt so much older than my peers who seemed to take so much of life for granted. I came to school here with so much understanding of the history of race in America and not enough understanding of class. My first women's studies class is taught by white woman writer Tillie Olsen and she more so than anyone who has taught me here understands the meaning of class powerlessness. Still she does not really think about race. She thinks everything is class and then maybe gender. In her class I struggle to speak my awareness against the insistence that being female is all that matters.

When I speak everyone stops to listen but then no one hears. They are all white and they are all here to celebrate being female. They do not want to hear that the shared reality of femaleness does not mean an equal share in powerlessness. There are no southern white girls. If there are, they remain silent. For no one who grows up in the apartheid south believes that the lot of black women and white women is the same, not even those who share the same class. Race makes the difference. And it is enough of a difference to preclude the possibility of common oppression.

They listen to me but they don't hear. They don't have to hear. This is what it means to be among the colonizers, you do not have to listen to what the colonized have to say, especially if their ideas come from experience and not from books. They ask you if there is a book they can read that will explain what you are talking about. I can hear everything the white girls who are my roommates and my peers are saying about the condition of women, can read my tattered copy of Simone de Beauvoir and be down with the discussion. When it comes to thinking about the intersection of race and gender I stand alone.

That is until I return home. And then I can be with him and he understands. To begin with he hears my pain at being silenced, not heard. He listens to my frustration when I want to write papers on black women and slavery, black women and domestic violence, black women and sexual liberation, and can find hardly anything. He listens to my rage. And never does he try to pretend there is no reason for rage. But he knows, he is older and has been more places and seen more in this world so he knows that rage is not enough. Again and again he says to me "If you want to read books that focus on black women, you better start writing and keep writing."

I come home one day and announce that I cannot return to class anymore. It's too much. I am too much on the outside. I am writing my book. Naturally, it will look at black women and feminism. In all my women's studies classes I grow weary of white women suggesting black women have always been free. This is because the white girls of my generation have read Betty Friedan and believe that work is all—that it will both save and liberate them. I have seen black women do nothing but work every day of very long lives and still end up with nothing, no freedom, no salvation, nothing. I am not convinced that work will save us. I know that black women are not free, that we do not have the feminist consciousness that we spend so much time talking about in these classes. No one wants to hear me tell them that these strong black women, these matriarchal folks they read about in sociology magazines, are tired of working and want more than anything to live in a world where their prince will come and take care of them. This is no dream black women have repudiated, they simply live in despair of that dream coming true so they do what they must to survive. I say they because I do not have this dream—never had.

Maybe because I had a daddy who provided, who was head of the household, who was always a churchgoing, hardworking, much of a man daddy and I understood the meaning of male domination in patriarchal society up close and personal. I saw early on that there was a price to be paid for being taken care of. I also knew from looking across the street that black women on welfare raising children alone paid a price and those who went out to work every day in the service of white folks who could humiliate them at will paid a price. None of these women were free. The only black women I knew growing up who had some control over their destinies were the schoolteachers who were single, childless, and owned their own property. I never thought about the place of love in their lives but I overheard the gossip about the men they would sometimes see and, in rare cases, the women. But free, black women were no more free than white women. It never ceased to amaze me that the white girls in my classes were so willing to insist on our freedom when there were no black females teaching us, sitting next to them in their classes, or living in their neighborhoods. As for the books black women writers had written, they had not read them. So much for common oppression and common understanding.

I often wondered where they encountered these liberated black women—in their dreams and fantasies of mammy and Aunt Jemima. In my freshman year of college, before I came to live with Mack I lived in a dormitory cleaned by black women working as maids. When I had no money to return home at the holidays I would go to their houses. One of them would always tell me *Don't let those white girls turn you into mammy. You are not there to take care of them, you there to get yours.* Mine was my freedom, which working black folks believed came through education. And so when those girls would talk about the strong free black matriarchs I just saw them longing for a world where they would not have to do anything, or give anything to the struggle to liberate black women.

Mind you there are plenty of black females who think the same way these girls and our teachers think, that black women are already free because so many of us work, pay the rent, and are in charge. This is no vision of freedom. I will not accept it. I have seen that work is not enough. It is part of the freedom process but not enough. The fact that all the white females at Stanford pretended not to have a clue about the difference between their lives and the lives of black females angered me but it did not turn me away from feminist thinking. My feminist resistance was born in the heart of that all-black patriarchal household and world I was raised in. I knew that I was there in feminist movement to claim all that was mine.

Those were the days when I moved off campus and lived with a white roommate, Mindy, a perfect privileged white girl who took nothing seriously. Trying to understand our differences kept me always looking at what it means to be black and female. Sitting in those classes where no one seemed to have a clue about the real lives of black women kept me standing in front of the mirror asking myself to make clear who I am black and female. Toni Cade's anthology *The Black Woman* answers some of my questions. All the writing brings race and gender together. There are stories of challenge and resistance. The words of black women demanding change light my path. I am not walking in the darkness alone. In *Ain't I Woman: Black Women and Feminism* I want to take the discussion further—want to offer more love and light.

Of course when I tell him I'm ready to write my book, he tells me It's about time. He does not say anything stupid like you are only nineteen, who are you to write a book, or who is going to read your book, or who will publish it. He just encourages me to write. I think and write. I tell him my book is a speculative book, that I am not trying to write a scholarly treatise. I am taking bits and pieces, fragments from everything and putting them together. Every day I search for books to read. I read two and three books a day, sometimes finding just a sentence that says something about black women, or something to back up an idea that I have. He shelves books in the library at the Hoover Institute, bringing home material I would not be able to find.

More than anybody in my life Mack understands the importance of my writing this book. He knows it will change life for me, give me a foundation. I need to center myself. He helps me in any way he can. He listens. He disagrees. I wake him up in the middle of the night and say things like If women slaves are having their periods and working in the fields wearing hardly any clothes with little access to soap and water just in this basic physical way slavery must have been fundamentally different for women than men. Or I wake him up to say I can't find anything that documents black males being raped as slaves even though there are other accounts of slavery in the world where this is documented. This is another way that a distinction is made between the lot of black female slaves and black males. I wake him up night after night with my thoughts. We talk them over. Sometimes he pleads Can't this wait until morning. Often he awakens in the middle of the night and finds me sitting at my desk in my study writing down thoughts I don't want to forget. I'm writing this book in the twilight. For in the day I am a student who must write papers, a worker who must earn money to pay the rent. We never have enough money. When it comes time to graduate I have not finished my book. I don't care about marching. Everything that matters is inside me. I am simply glad school is over. He on the other hand has a dissertation to write. I wait for the darkness and stillness of night—for twilight mind to give me waking dreams—new ways to look at black women's place in the world.

14

Poetry sustains life. Of this I am certain. There is no doubt in my mind that the pain of poverty whether material or emotional lack can be eased by the power of language. I know this intimately. For in that misunderstood childhood of mine, I found that sanctuary in poetry. It restored me, allowed me to come back from the space of woundedness and sadness to a recognition of beauty. Growing up in a working-class black southern home, in racial segregation, I moved beyond the boundaries of race and class through books. The writers of my earliest reading days were not African American for I had been given a collection of more than a hundred little leather-bound books with tiny print that you could hold in the palms of your hands. And these books were classic or so the elderly neighbor told me who had called me to come to her house and get them.

She was not even ten years old. Yet she would lie in her bed upstairs by the window reading Keats, Shelley, and Wordsworth, reading Robert Browning and Elizabeth Barrett Browning. In her dark hours she loved to just contemplate the line a thing of beauty is a joy for ever: its loveliness increases. *And to say aloud to herself* yes, in spite of it all, some shape of beauty moves away the pall from our dark spirits. *She did ask her mama to explain what it means* I love thee to the depth and breadth and height My soul can reach, when feeling out of sight For the ends of Being and ideal Grace.

Mama nurtured my love of poetry, my love of reading, my desire to write as though it was a tender plant she wanted to give all the sunshine and water that would be necessary to make it grow. And then when she thought all that reading and thinking was making me strange, setting me apart, making me unfit for marriage, she tried to make this passion less intense, to cool my ardor. Then she could be cruel and unyielding, threatening to take away those books if I did not get my head out of the clouds and come right back down to earth where I belonged. Poor mama, I did not even begin understand her conflict until I sat in that packed room with all those other female bodies listening to Tillie Olsen talk about the anguish of trying to choose between mothering and being a good wife and writing.

Her mama used to always tell them that she had loved reading when she was in school. That they inherited their love of reading and writing from her. At college she realized how young her mama was when she had had her first child. At her predominantly white prestigious college she thought about the fact that her mama had not finished high school. She only learned this when her mama, as a grown woman, began to study to pass the test for equivalency.

I sat in Tillie Olsen's class and wept when she talked about how raising children made it so hard to find the time to read and write. I thought about mama and how much of her young life had been given over to just that and I longed to give her back those years when her imagination was full and fresh and longing to create worlds. Of course when I try to express my sorrow and regret to mama later that night she acts as though she does not understand what I am talking about. She soothes my heartache by insisting that her life has been just as she always dreamed of it being—having a good husband and provider, raising children. I am not fooled by her insistence that life has been the way she dreamed it would be.

I know she dreamed of love and marriage. I know she had her moments of happiness. But I was there when the lights went out of her eyes, when love betrayed her for the last time. In the shadows of that betrayal she must have imagined the path her life would have taken had she been free to study and grow and learn before becoming a mother so young, so many times. In Tillie Olsen's class I come to understand why mama seems so determined to control my destiny and the destiny of her other five daughters. She wants us to have a full and complete life. She does not want us to miss out on anything, not love or marriage or children or poetry. Still, she is not certain that it is good for a woman to know too much, to be too smart. She is proud of her smart daughter even as she fears for her.

Daddy put it in her head that the reason this smart child was so foolish and hardheaded was cause she was reading all them books and spending all that time keeping to herself. That's when Rosa Bell began to yell at her to put that book down, get your head out of that book and get some fresh air. They moved from the house on First Street when she was away at college. And when she asked what had happened to the beloved books of her childhood, mama said That mess—we threw most of it away. It was as though they had thrown away the part of her past that they feared the most, the words inside those strange books. She felt it was their final rejection of her— the real her.

When I met Mack he courted me (even though he was still living with a girlfriend) by sending me poems, words he had written in tiny handwriting as difficult and as hard to read as my own. The first one was unsigned. It was a poem inspired by me, about me. I was too thrilled for words. It had the line *and her voice, if at all she spoke, it sang*. I discover myself in poetry. He understands that.

Poetry is the place of transcendence. No wonder then that before feminism I never really thought much about race and gender. Even as kid when I played that card game Authors, I always thought about the stern, somewhat sad look on Emily Dickinson's face. That her face was white, that she was the only female in the group, never bothered me. I just didn't think about it. And even though I read all these writers who were white I never thought about race. It was the words that mattered and the feelings the words created that meant something. Poetry is the place of transcendence.

At some point though she realizes she is not reading any African American writers. Somewhere in her subconscious she realizes that if she can find no black writers then maybe there is no space for her. In high school she goes to the library and finds James Weldon Johnson's The Book of American Negro Poetry. *This is poetry her family likes to hear and she can recite it to them all day and all night long. She loves this book so much she never returns it to the library. The words of these poets are just that precious.*

I don't know what made me keep that anthology of American Negro poetry. All I knew was that I had to have it in my possession, to concretely remind me that this wonderful poetry coming from our life existed. I memorized those poems. Georgia Douglas Johnson's *I want to die while you love me,* oh! *who would care to live till love has nothing more to ask, and nothing more to give.* When I look for more of her work in the card catalog I find nothing. James Weldon Johnson and Langston Hughes are the writers I find. Their words speak to me so deeply, I am overjoyed. At church, at school, I am always reciting their work. This time I notice that there are only five or six women writers in an anthology with lots of men. I don't think about why that is—just take note of it. Of course, one day I intend to be one of those women poets in the anthology.

She packs for college and takes two books, Rilke's Letters to a Young Poet *and* The Book of American Negro Poetry. *Feeling guilty she thinks about giving the poetry book back to the library. But she can't. It's the symbol of her yearning to find a voice. That's what her writing classes in college are making her think about—the uniqueness of her voice. She goes to the library and listens to poets reading their work. She listens to herself reading. She listens to poets reading here and there. It's a new world. Poetry that is no longer private but out there in the world.*

At Stanford the poetry reading that inspires me the most is given by a little short white woman poet Adrienne

110

Rich. She has long been one of my favorites. Before the reading I can't believe I am going to see her in the flesh. I feel as excited as I did before having sex for the first time, a woman writer, a poet in the flesh. Believe it or not, I think she will have all the answers. She will be the living embodiment of all that Sylvia Plath is not. I can't wait to hear her.

When they go to the Adrienne Rich reading, the room is packed. She pushes her way through the crowd to be near the front. She is practically sitting at Rich's feet. He stands in the back. This is not one of his favorite poets and not his scene. When Rich begins to read her voice is so bitter it stuns this innocent listener. Frightened by what she hears, by what Rich has to say about women writers, she is wounded. The poet's words fill her with doubt, make her think that after all there is no need to write, for no one will value and hear her words. Afterwards she is too shy to ask questions, too afraid of rejection. The next day she calls the home of the professor where Rich is staying to see if the author is willing to talk. The anonymous voice on the phone dismisses her request as absurd—firmly dismissing her with the question Don't you understand how precious a writer's time is.

This is the only living well-known woman poet she has ever heard. The sound of Adrienne Rich's voice was filled with a pain that strikes her heart. Is this pain all that women writers are able to speak? And is death the only outcome of too much yearning for expression? What are

111

the conditions that will allow women writers to live and write? She goes back to Virginia Woolf, to A Room of Her Own, *to find solace—to find answers.*

The other book I took with me when I left home for the first time was a tattered worn paperback copy of Rainer Maria Rilke's *Letters to a Young Poet*. This book charts the poet's journey for me. It was given to me by a white female college student at a retreat for Campus Crusade for Christ. Her name is Annell St. Charles. She gave it to me after I read one of my poems at an evening session. My poems are all about death and dying—all sad. She gives me this with the dedication that says *to one who sees with an eye for the inner life*. Little does she know how much this book will comfort and sustain me. I read and reread it as life at home becomes unbearable and I dream of ending my life, of exiting. How soothing to read Rilke: *learning time is always a long secluded time, and so loving, for a long while ahead and far on into life, is— solitude, intensified and deepened longness for him who loves. Love is at first not anything that means merging, giving over, and uniting with another (for what would a union be of something unclarified and unfinished still subordinate)—it is a high inducement to the individual to ripen, to become something in himself, to become world, to become world for himself, for another's sake, it is a great exacting claim upon him, something that chooses him out and calls him to vast things*. For my lonely heart Rilke has no race, no gender, not even his different

112

nationality matters, he offers solace, the possibility of a life lived in devotion to writing.

Mack reads Rilke. Most women writers cannot hold his attention with the exception of the strange and compelling H.D. (Hilda Doolittle). He was well into her poems before he knew he was reading a woman. Mack and I never discuss whether he thinks women writers are as good or as important as men. It's clear that I love male writers as much as I love female writers, but he has a literary hierarchy. The writers he admires most are men, and not just any man, the difficult ones. We do a literary magazine together and call it *Hambone*. When we first begin, I work as hard on the magazine as he does but he takes all the credit. This does not bother me, I'm not into public stuff or putting my name on stuff. It's his project and he loves it best. Later though, long after we have left Stanford where the magazine first began, he claims it for himself alone and pushes me in the background in more ways than one.

More and more we live as though poetry is his turf and I am writing elsewhere. That makes it easier it seems. He gets to be seen as the real artist "the poet" and I get be this writer who is doing feminist theory. In my life poetry returns to the place it inhabited in childhood. It is the writing I do in private, not in secret but in private. Although it remains the primary passion of my writing life, I don't know much about poetics. I read poems. Mack knows more and speaks about poetics with an authority that I cannot claim. I learn from him.

Intuitively I sense that I have nothing to offer the discussion of poetics which captivates him.

His favorite living poet is Robert Duncan whose poems enchant us both. Mack is a devoted reader of Duncan's work and writes critical work about his poetry. I am just a mere lover of the poems. I cannot speak that love in any way that is meaningful. Robert Duncan comes into our life like a whirlwind, embodying the passion for poetry that we feel is the heartbeat of our life together. Duncan talks and talks. We are more than willing to listen. Mack fascinates Duncan. I am someone he rarely looks at or speaks to. That's fine because I am more interested in the poetry than the man. How those lines *often I am permitted to return to a meadow* enchant me. Even though I am practically invisible to this man whose eyes make you think he will never see straight I am grateful to be in his presence and hear him speak. He makes a life lived in and through poetry a path to the ecstatic. We love to read him—to hear him read. This poet who can write without apology or shame: *For this is the company of the living and the poet's voice speaks from no crevice in the ground between mid-earth and underworld breathing fumes of what is deadly to know, news larvae in tombs and twists of time to feed upon, but from the hearth stone, the lamp light, the heart of the matter where the house is held.* We are transported to another place when we hear him read. Poetry is the place of transcendence.

15

He thinks I am arrogant about writing, crazy to not be so interested in what other people think of my words. These words are written for me, I tell him. I feel it is I who must learn how to stand at a distance and judge them—that only then can I make sense of the judgments of others. When he hands me a poem to read I am reluctant to share immediate thoughts, criticism. Poetry—a poem—is something I have to live with for a long time before I begin to have something to say. I want to live with the poem, to hold it close. In his eyes my slow response is a sign of lack of interest.

He thinks of her as a naïve artist, someone painting from intuition—someone who has the feel for where words can be placed, who is interested in feelings. Superior to her he is interested in the complexity of language. That's how he

sees himself superior to her. She does not understand that
he thinks of himself as Pygmalion, of her as his pupil—his
little southern primitive whom he can teach about civi-
lization, high culture, and what really matters.

I like to love a man who can teach me things. I read
everything he reads. He is older, has been out in the
world more, has traveled. I have hardly been on a city
bus. Escalators are foreign and scary. Elevators have no
place in my life. More than anything I simply desire to
stay home—to read and to write. He teaches me that it is
important to go places in the world, to experience more,
to write more.

We go to poetry readings. Like a nomadic tribe that
moves with our favorite things, we are following always in
the shadows of other poets. We will sit at the feet of the
Russian poet at City Lights Bookstore in San Francisco so
packed with people that we can smell each other, that
bodies must be moved so as not to be a fire hazard. There
are protesters screaming in the back and we are seeing
that poetry is political in a different way in other coun-
tries. We know this but today we are feeling it—as there
is a moment of fear so electric it moves through the
crowd, like a lightning bolt shattering everyone's glasslike
heart. For a moment we are all that is fragile in this room.

In this space we are surrounded by white people. We
are always the only dark people we see. Everyone stares
at us. When I want to know, why do they look so hard—
what is it they see, I am told that we are such a striking

116

couple, this dark black man who looks like a Benin sculpture in his skullcaps and his goatee. This petite brown-skinned woman with hair that falls around her face like a halo. *And your clothes they are always so interesting, both of you. You are strange, exotic, beautiful. You should enjoy it when we stare.* I never say when white people look too long, too hard, something in me becomes afraid. Here in this crowded room, where we are still as only the voice of poetry speaks, we forget the colors and cultures that do not bind us. We live for a time in a world of words. We are collectively spellbound. It is a moment of shared ecstasy.

Poetry is the heartbeat of our love. We go everywhere to listen to poets. He has written a dissertation on the Black Mountain School. For him, I labor over Charles Olson and come to love his words only when I memorize the poems and hear them, really hear the lyricism in the words: *As the dead lay upon us, they are the dead in ourselves. Disentangle the nets of being.* No day goes by in our life that we are not hearing some line of poetry together.

Her country schools were really places where education was behind the times. And in some ways that was good. Like in all education for racial uplift in the all-black schools she attended there had always been an emphasis on communication, on reciting. Early in Booker T. Washington School they would be given long poems to recite. She learned to stand before hundreds of her peers

117

and read poems with meaning. She loves to give him poetry, to recite for him as they lie in the dark in the sweaty aftermath of sex. Language and eros. There will never be a separation in her mind. They make one another happen.

I imagine Emily Dickinson living alone, untouched by any hand save her own, but still claiming a world of passion. Had I not grown up in the closed world of heavy-handed church doctrine and still found a way to reach my body in the dark. Those "wild nights" of Dickinson's imagination were there in her real moments of sleeplessness, of lying awake in a world where your own body is your own body to claim, in words, in its nakedness that is there only for you to know, to see, to enjoy.

I write better when I am shut away, confined. To be closed in is sometimes a comfort. It makes you hear in the stillness every sound in the words you write. Whether I write poetry or prose I will be speaking words to myself in that closed off world where only my ears can hear. Reading poetry to others is fine but not my poetry. I have no need to share these words. Anyway I write mostly about death. And who finds death interesting.

We believe in ourselves as poets more than we believe in our love.

16

We decide to move away from Palo Alto, from Stanford and all that is comfortable and familiar to us. Berkeley is the place I like the most, filled with bookstores and little clothing boutiques and places to eat. Berkeley is the place where it's fine to be political, to be upset about racism, sexism, and everything else that is fucking up the planet. We cannot afford Berkeley. We find a place in Oakland, a huge second-floor flat with tons of space a room for me and a room for Mack, more space than we know what to do with. I have to find a job. There is never any doubt about my working. I want to work—to pay my way. I work the same amount of time as he does and am getting paid less. It pisses me off every time I think about anybody thinking that work will liberate.

On a cold Monday morning I stand in a long line of females waiting to interview for the phone company which needs operators. When my turn comes I know how to act not too stupid and not too smart. I know to make it seem that my having gone to Stanford was a mistake and that really I intend to stay at the phone company forever. I begin with the graveyard shift. Getting home at night is a drag if Mack can't pick me up but I find a way, sometimes I take the bus, sometimes I hitch a ride, and sometimes I walk. The office where we, mostly women, mostly black, work has no windows. Little things like that enrage me, no windows anywhere. When we need to go to the ladies' room we have to watch the little red light to make sure no one else is gone. Everything here is about surveillance. We are checked constantly, evaluated, and some of us are fired. I am good at my job and never fear that I will be let go. None of the higher-ups knows how much I hate it. They are thinking I can be one of the "girls" to be groomed for management. I sit at my desk dreaming of ways to blow up the building and they think I could rise in the company. The phone company sucks.

I love the women I work with. They almost all have children. A lot of them come from the south just like me. We understand one another. When I tell them about the book I am writing they urge me to tell our story. No one minds when I interview them about our lives, the way we live, the way we love. No one here thinks that we are liberated. We joke constantly about being one paycheck away from nothing. Everyone knows I will leave this job eventually. I tell them how much I want to be a writer, how I write when I get home from work, no matter how tired I am. I write to know that I am not a disembodied voice chained to a computer. Those of us who work the graveyard shift are a special breed. We work without the busyness and comforts of the day. The office is silent and dimly lit. But we can get away with more. That's what it's all about for us, letting the phone company know we can find a way to play and enjoy ourselves even though the rules would keep us working and working with no time to know one another. Sometimes we visit each other on our off days but mostly we spend time together at work— listening to each other's stories. Mostly we talk about not having enough money, and not having enough love. Sometimes I work so hard, such long hours, I feel there is no time to think. I have to stop work to think, to have time to write. Only I can't stop work.

He's writing. He's doing his dissertation. By the time I come home from work, he's done. We don't talk much about his process. His ways of working impress me, make me feel inadequate. Mack sits long hours at his desk and works in a diligent disciplined manner. I want so badly to work this way. But I just can't. Even when I force myself, I don't get enough done. It's just me staring at the blank page.

Both of us handwrite everything. We both have tiny handwriting. We both use notebooks where we write our thoughts and ideas. We never invade each other's private space so I never know what's in his notebooks and he never knows what I am writing. I keep a journal—but for me it's a working journal. The place where I record ideas, write fragments of work I will use later, where I write about what I am reading, and sometimes where I record the mundane. I try hard to work like he works and I never get it right until I find my way.

Trying to work long hours helps me to find my way. Since there are only a few hours when I am not really tired, I discover I work best in a short space of time. It is so exciting that I am finally finding my own style of working. Intense concentration in short periods of time is the best way for me to work. I no longer try to work for hours. I try instead to write a page or a couple of paragraphs and then stop. I want to play the rest of the time. To play I visit with Jettie B. the older black southern woman who lives downstairs from us with her husband and who is always cooking something good. We compete to see who is the better cook. Of course my mama is the best cook. Mama is fantastic. I am still just learning. I like to shop—buying things for the flat. I talk with Jettie about the book I am writing. She works as a maid. She has no need to work. She does it for the extra money. Jettie B. wants me to wear makeup and straighten my hair. She reminds me of mama and my sisters. Mack has no interest in meeting neighbors. He likes to keep to himself. I want to know everything about the world around me. I talk to everybody and everybody talks to me. It's a way of living in the world that makes me feel safe.

Mack looks down on people, judging them more by what they think and what they know rather than what's inside their hearts. He does not have the time to look inside anyone's heart. He's busy writing his dissertation and trying to keep a space for his own work to evolve. Sometimes he sits for hours and writes only a sentence— and for him that is enough. When I write nothing for hours it depresses me and it takes a longer time for me to come back to the page and work.

Other than the few southern black folks I meet, I am not accustomed to getting close to strangers. It disturbs me. Growing up we never visited anyone hardly except family. We never went eating out. Daddy used to say, When we are living with the best cook in the world, why would we ever want to eat out. We are serious about the meaning of home. Home is where loved ones and loved things are. It is not the place you bring anything unsavory—that's the word my mother had used. Even though I am in college far away from the south, from my people, I don't want just anyone to come to my house— to be among my things.

Although Rosa Bell, her mama, feels that she should have rid herself of those backwoods ways a long time ago, it's still in her. She's the one that taught them children not to be running here and there with just anybody. It comes from that secret pain in her own life. Rosa Bell never talks about her past, her girlhood. Yet she tells them to keep to themselves, to be each other's best friends. They some well-mannered kids. You never see them fussing and fightin' cause Rose (nobody ever calls her Rosa) and Mr.

Veodis, they don't allow that. Everybody know that Mr. Veodis is that silent type of man, the kinda man you don't mess with, cause "still waters run deep." And she done come to college and got a man just like Mr. Veodis but she don't see it—not yet.

In social settings I am awkward. How can we be real with so many strangers. How can we smile and tell the truth to so many people we don't know. Small talk makes me feel the way I do when a mosquito is buzzing around my head—irritated—and then finally unable to get any relief I just slaughter the damn thing. I slaughter the moment by saying something real. Everybody acts like I can't see that they think I am strange and out of place like some antique in a room full of modern furniture. I don't care what they think—they are not real to me, just ghosts that have nothing to do with my life.

17

Her mama used to say to her practically every time she got mad, which was often, practically every time she whipped her, which was often: *You ought to care what folks think. I care.* Perhaps if she, the daughter, had had words then, she would have talked about going to school with those red marks all over her body, little welts from where the switches had stung her flesh, and being made fun of. She would have talked about sitting right there in front of everybody in Miss Hamby's history class and crying for no reason at all that anybody could see. And everyone thinking she was strange. Inside she felt awkward. She never went anywhere much or did anything much. She had friends but she was never able to run with them, to hang, mama always set the limits. Mostly she hid in her room knowing that if she went out something would go wrong and she would be punished. When your mama is whipping you and telling you *I will break you*

and Don't make me kill you and you are just desperate
enough, just one time to fight back and scream with rage I
don't have a mama. And you see that you have hurt her
(whom you long to protect from every pain) but you got
to let her know that you are your own person, how can
you care what folks thousands of miles from where you
are born who have never even given you eye water to cry
with think about you.

I can tell he is not pleased when we go out. I am failing
him not even coming close to being the perfect little academic wife. Sometimes I try and sometimes I don't. It is
hard for me. I am not used to crossing the boundaries of
race—and by and large white folk don't interest me—
least of all the kind of white people we meet in the academic world. White folks we meet in the world of poetry
always seem to be beyond whiteness. With them I am not
strange. Only his career is not being forged there in the
world of poetry it is forged in the university, a setting that
has no meaning for me. Books and learning have
meaning and that can come to you anywhere. I am in college because I need a job. He is here to be a professor.
He knows how to conduct himself.

Again and again I am at a loss for words at these functions. I don't understand bourgeois decorum. It hurts me
to lie and to be lied to. All manner of fake and phoniness
unsettles my heart. I am constantly looking behind the
words they say and looking into their hearts. Often what I
see frightens, leaves me without words. Only Mack
understands how much this world is driving me crazy.

And I begin to drive him crazy. He teaches me the rules but I do not understand. Or I refuse to play.

It's not that he's indifferent. He knows she will get hurt, be battered and bruised by this world in ways that she can't even begin to see or fathom. When he tries to protect her, she resists. Headstrong she will go her way. And he lets her go even though he will have to pick up the pieces in the end. She does not see how wedded to the system he is—that she is the voice of his rebellion. He is not a rebel. Caught up in the arrogance and ignorance of her youth she cannot see that.

White people are always choosing which one of us they like. Usually, they choose him. In their imaginations he is the ultimate exotic Negro—one who looks black, real black, yet personifies white notions of rationality, decorum, civilization. I am in their eyes the primitive. I talk about being black, curse, talk loudly, speak bluntly. When he goes to his first assistant professor job (deciding that he has to leave California and go to Wisconsin) I agree to come along. I am sick of my job at the phone company and know it's time to go back to school. I hate school but I hate dead-end jobs more. We talk about marriage. He's not sure he wants to start out his career with confusion about whether I am his partner or his wife. I don't want to marry but I want to be with Mack. I agree to come along even though my heart tells me we will never be happy there. I don't always follow my heart. Sometimes I follow him.

Since I don't drive he must do all the work. We cross the country in his tiny dark blue Volkswagen Bug filled with our belongings. We listen to music, talk about everything we've never talked about before in great detail. I hate travel but it feels good to be on the road finding out who we are together. He knows that I am afraid of life in Wisconsin. I want to be a person who can embrace change although there is a part of me that always wants life to stay the same, not to change. We arrive in Wisconsin sick of being together, disagreeing about the future. Staying with faculty members who see me as the wife, we pretend that's who I am. Although later that will cause problems because of financial aid when colleagues challenge my right to receive a stipend since my "husband" makes so much money.

In graduate school everything about me is wrong: the way I dress, the way I talk, the way I do my papers, the way I am too affectionate, the way I do not accept the hierarchy (too much challenging of my superiors). Mack no longer tries to correct me. He lets me pay for my mistakes. He no longer picks up the pieces. His attention is focused on his career—on writing. As long our sex life is great he does not care what I do or who I hang out with.

Whenever there are departmental functions I go with him, playing the role of the subordinate wife. I have learned to cook and can cook anything, from anywhere in the world. This pleases him and his colleagues. I cook and cook it seems. He stills smokes a lot of dope and hangs out with the fringe thinkers who do the same, who want to be writers too. In the wee hours of the night I open my

Simone Beck cookbook and spend hours making the perfect *marquis de chocolat*. Our house is a place where folks congregate and eat. Even though I sometimes choose the people they are almost always more interested in him.

It's like they live two lives. In one they are pretending to be the perfect couple dominant man submissive woman. In the other, the one that takes place in the shadows where few people can see what's going on, they act autonomously. In that space she is writing her poems, her books, slowly emerging as the intellectual she longs to be. In the space he encourages and supports, he is still her best friend. But when it comes to the world of academe she falls short and he is beginning to think that she could possibly hurt his career, hurt his chances of smoothly arriving at where he wants to go. She has already come to see that he is a green light person. For him things have always been easy, few obstacles in his way. She on the other hand is always having to confront red lights. There is always something in her path that has to be overcome. Still they have a good life together—a warm and intense life.

Eventually we decide that as a place to put down roots Wisconsin is not for us—way too cold, not enough black folks, and much too conventional ways of thinking about life and relationships. We decide to go back to California.

He chooses Southern California where he has grown up, where his people are, where he will be near home. She has to learn how to drive. He tries to teach her and fails. She cannot concentrate for fear of doing the wrong thing and making him angry. She does the wrong thing anyway. He is angry. She goes to a driving school. It takes her a long—long—time to be comfortable. They have traded in the faithful blue bug for two Volkswagen Rabbits, hers is red and his is white. They live in a beautiful duplex in Hollywood on Alta Vista. It's owned by Integral Yoga. They take yoga classes and become vegetarians and make new friends. She works at the Bodhi Tree, a fancy new age bookstore, that is until she is let go for reasons that are never clear, only that she has the wrong attitude and does not mix well with the mood and vibe of the store. Once again she failed to get along with the group. She talks too much about new age fascism, about who gets the money and where it goes.

They move again. This time to an Orthodox Jewish neighborhood. Their landlady, who lives on the bottom floor, never stops telling them how no one wants her to rent to blacks. She visits the landlady regularly and listens to her story and her grief. She listens to the stories of the old days, back in the old country, when life was good. It reminds her some of how she feels about life in Kentucky. She knows all the children in the neighborhood and her favorite one lives next door. It's good, the life they have created.

Although she left Wisconsin with a master's, she is now in a Ph.D. program at USC where he teaches. He is in black studies and English—the combination works best. It gives him more freedom. She teaches courses in black *studies. Her first course is on black women. The class is mobbed. She is afraid but eager to do her job. Women's studies did not want to offer her course. In the English department everyone agrees that she would do well to focus her attention more on graduate school than writing a book about black women that no one wants to read. Black studies is a haven.*

Finally I finish my book *Ain't I a Woman: Black Women and Feminism.* I send it to publisher after publisher. They reject it. I am devastated. I lie on the cool wood floor and weep. Rejection makes me feel everyone was right and no one wants to know about black women. I put the book in a closet. Mack gives me sympathy but his attention is on his own work as he will be up for tenure soon. Now my attention is all on graduate school. I still write but I write in the shadows—doing my poetry in the wee hours when I am not working, or doing school, or making bread, or cooking dinners for friends.

Mack is growing tired of my failures. He thinks I complicate life by refusing to play by the rules. He thinks I do not understand the meaning of compromise. Sometimes he reminds me of mama and daddy. Sometimes he is all too quick to punish and say I told you so. I am not happy. I am always sad. I see a psychiatrist. He tells me I am suffering from acute depression. That I've been suffering from depression for most of my life. He wants to give me drugs. I stop seeing him. The nightmares I am having do not go away. The problems at school continue. Everything I do is wrong.

She fights with the most powerful professors. She has no idea that they are waiting for that moment when they can annihilate her. Their weapon is exclusion. They definitely intend to see that she does not leave this university with a Ph.D. She has been talked to about her decorum, about not having the proper demeanor of a graduate student. Things are better for a time, after she takes a leave of absence. They do not know that she "paused" because she had become so obsessed with the idea of entering the office of one white male professor who seemed to feel that it was his particular destiny to humiliate and break white women and all people of color.

I dreamed of entering his office with a gun, of ordering him to sit down in that calm clean clear rational voice of fascist control he is so fond of using. I would begin to calmly discuss the way he speaks to us, the sexist, racist, antihomosexual jokes he tells. When he pleads with me to be calm and understanding, I respond in the same tones he is so fond of using when dehumanizing and crushing us. I assure him that by encouraging him to stop teaching the way he has consistently encouraged me and other students like me to leave graduate school I really have his best interests at heart. As he was fond of telling me *Not everyone is cut out for graduate school.* As I point my gun directly in his face, ready to pull the trigger, I fondly tell him Not everyone is cut out for teaching. I have this fantasy so often, it worries me. I feel I am on the verge of

132

a nervous breakdown so I drop his class, the one everyone must take to graduate. I come back another semester and say nothing. He is pleased and smiles at me all semester.

I pass hours of written exams. My orals take place in a small room with five white people present. When I am asked how I will teach James Joyce, I respond that I have no intention of teaching his work and give my reasons why. I am totally honest. I make it clear that I have read Joyce but am unmoved by his writing and that of many of the so-called great white male writers. I speak about the need to have an unbiased curriculum, one that is diverse and varied. Since I have so clearly read everything required of me and indicate that in the discussion, I believe I have done well. When they tell me with smiles that I have failed, that I can try again in so many months, I am stunned. I know I will never willingly face them again.

She learned the hard way that if those in power who can decide your fate do not like you they will punish you. All that time she believed justice and fair play would override feelings of personal dislike. She did not understand that they felt people like her, black people, Negroes, niggers, should be glad they finally opened up their all-white schools and let them in, how dare the darkies come in and be disobedient. That's what they meant when they told her she did not have the proper demeanor of a graduate student. By the time she walked the short distance home from the exams, brushing the tears from her eyes, she understood the way the system worked and was reconciled. She would have to start over somewhere else.

Her one graduate school buddy, Mary, another black woman, expected she would fail. She knew how much they disliked her because they were always asking Mary why can't she more like you. Mary was the kind of person who did not make waves. She did as she was told. She swallowed her rage. Like other graduate students she knew how to fake and how to pretend. She knew that they hated to see black women so smart, so sure of themselves. Mary knew that they were just waiting to cut her down, to annihilate her.

The truth really was that they had no desire to annihilate her. They just wanted to show her how the system worked. They wanted to teach her to surrender and submit. They just wanted her to conform, to show the proper respect. They just wanted to see her obey.

Mack was waiting to hear the outcome. He was not surprised that they had failed her. He knew how the system worked. But there was not much for him to say. She told the news calmly—quietly—then did not speak of it again that night. She went to her room to be alone, to think, to gather her thoughts. He respected that.

I was disappointed. But that feeling was overshadowed by the recognition of the strength of my idealism. I was shocked that I had really believed a spirit of justice and fair play would prevail. I was awed by my innocence. How could I have thought that I could speak truth to power and not be punished.

134

18

Every month when my period comes I am sick as a dog. I bleed so much. No matter how many pads I wear and how often I change them, blood is everywhere. He hates the times that I am sick. I hate having sex when I am bleeding. He likes fucking during that time. He likes that mixture of semen and blood. I know though that he will not clean the sheets. That will be my task. I am always so sick during this time, I just want to be left alone. At first he tries to be understanding and then he can't understand why it hurts so much. Other women he knows have no menstrual pain. I think he should go and live with those women then. They are women I envy. None of my sisters suffered as I suffered.

Maybe it was because there was never any meat on her bones. She was always so skinny. Even though her period came later than her sisters' she suffered more. They tried to strengthen her by making her eat, drink those drinks of milk and raw eggs. She never knew how much her mama worried that she was just not gonna make it. She had asthma real bad. And would sit up night after night struggling to breathe. They did not have money to be running back and forth to the doctor so they tried home remedies made of honey fresh from the honeycomb, special teas, and herbs. But she suffered. Being sick all the time just made her more of an outsider. To her sisters and brother she was a crybaby who was no fun.

Mack thinks I should exercise more. It's true that growing up with asthma, I have always shied away from intense exercise for fear it will bring on an attack. Even when I exercise more, the pain still comes. He keeps saying it's in my mind. And I am willing even to believe that if my mind can make the pain go away. I never want to travel for fear that I will be sick, that I will be bleeding heavily and soil everything. He just says It's a drag living with somebody who is sick every month. I take high-dosage birth control pills and they help. I feel like I'm addicted to them. Even though the doctors warn me about taking such a high dosage I am afraid to stop, afraid of the heavy bleeding and the pain.

Sometimes when it's that time of the month and I am grappling so with the bleeding and the pain, it's hard for me not to think that these biological differences make it hard for women to be the equals. The one small comfort is that I know not every female suffers the way I do. The doctors tell me if I have a child it will probably make things better. They tell me if I don't want to have children then I should just have a hysterectomy and forget about having periods all together.

I love children but the thought of carrying a child in my body frightens me. My body has always let me down in some way. Anyway he does not want to have children. And I would not have a child with a man who did not want to be a father, to really parent. Later when the doctors are urging me to stop taking the high-dosage pill we talk about whether Mack will have a vasectomy. He's not sure. We might break up. He might end up with a woman who wanted to have children. And I demand to know: You would have children you don't want to parent because some woman wanted you to. I am clear that I would never have children with Mack; that I would never want a child to be continually hurt by his indifference, his coldness. I think I can walk away from his moods but not a child. I think it would be a good idea for him to have a vasectomy—that's if he really believes he does not want to have children.

He goes without me to the clinic where they show him videos of men talking about vasectomies. His penis will need to be shaved. And that's where we leave it. Things are bad between us. We fight about money. We fight about me being sick. We fight about having sex. I come home from work one day and he tells me that he is thinking seriously about having a vasectomy. The next day I come home and he tells me that he has done it—

just like that—no discussion. I can't understand how he's left me out of such a major decision. It was his decision—he tells me. And anyway he says Aren't you the one who says this is your body and you do with it what you want to. He tells me about shaving his penis clean and shows it to me—not a trace of hair. The nurses he said could not believe it—how clean it was. They tell him most men come in and they have barely shaved or not at all. They are too afraid of using a razor on their private parts. I tease him that maybe they were really checking out his big dick.

I am frightened he made this decision without talking with me. Now he wants to behave as though we had already agreed it should happen, that it was no big deal. I feel it to be an act of aggression, the way he did it. He knows I am the one who is not sure about having babies. It's as though he's letting me know we will never bring any little black children into this world.

We fight about everything these days. Our fights are long quiet discussions. Every now and then they fill me with rage. I am sick of talking things over. The other day we were fighting about money, about other people. I jumped on him like a wild cat attacking prey hitting out wildly. He does not hit me back. I am no stranger to hitting. It does not frighten me to hit or be hit. Later I do see that it's stupid to jump somebody stronger than you. His arms are strong, he holds me down easily. He makes fun of my rage.

More and more I don't desire him. I continue to have sex with him and the sex is good but finding the place of desire within myself is hard. We are both writing. That makes it seem that life is still good, that everything is fine. Yet I think more and more that we are growing apart. There is a student in my class named Shane who disturbs me. He sits at the back of the class and rarely says anything. His counselor calls me to talk. Shane says I pick on him. I take this seriously and try to watch myself. I see what's happening. I'm attracted to him but must have used aggression not to see it. We talk. I don't say what the deal is. It's a night class. And now that we are on better terms he always waits till everyone leaves to walk me to my car. Sometimes we sit in the parking lot and talk. Sometimes we kiss. Neither of us is ready to go any further than this.

More and more my body seems like an alien thing I can't trust. Mack thinks that since he has had a vasectomy everything should be all right. I should want to have sex as much as he does. I stop taking the pill and use heavy-duty painkillers instead. My book is in the closet somewhere. And I don't think about it so much anymore. I work on writing poems. Writing is still the sweetest passion. Sometimes when we are having long intense hours of lovemaking, I am somewhere else writing, putting together words for the future. It is easier to understand women's liberation in the workplace, harder to understand what to do at home. Most of the women I know want to have sex less often than the men they live with. We talk about whether monogamy is the problem, living in couples. We talk and talk but it does not change anything.

19

I have no desire to own things. Giving things away is more fun. Belongings demand too much. People die for things. People kill the things they love rather than let them be free. In my extended family we are raised to kill whenever it is a matter of honor. Mama says this is that backwoods mess she has wanted to get away from all her life, the old ways. Mama wants me to be a child of the new. I am an affront to all her dreams because the backwoods speaks to me, is in my blood. The old ways call me.

Her mama believed she had learned all these foolish ways of thinking about life over home, over listening to Baba's stories. There was even a point in time when her mama thought she needed to forbid these wasteful conversations that were filling her daughter's head with crazy thoughts.

She felt the same way about all those books; that they were making this daughter unfit to live with other people, unfit for the real world.

In between conversations with old folks and time spent in books, she learned that her word was her bond— that power lay in being open and honest, telling the truth and bearing the responsibility of that truth. To have courage to live was to learn to be courageous about dying. She was not afraid of dying. She was not afraid to kill. Honor was worth dying for. These were the crazy ideas her mama wanted her to leave behind having seen too many folks cut and killed behind foolishness. There was nothing foolish about telling the truth and bearing responsibility for that truth. She was following that backwoods logic of making your own rules and laws and not caring what the world thought. Hypocrisy, her grandmother had said, was the real evil. To be humble was to know oneself fully.

There were times I felt as though I could not be mama's daughter. I was the child of another time, a child from the old world, the wilderness, the backwoods. A renegade horse. Over and over when I was whipped they would say I am going to break you. Whatever my spirit was it was not willing to be broken—it stood up, it fought back, and it paid the price.

She suffered in childhood. It was amazing that her spirit remained intact. They tried in every way to break her.

141

Sometimes it would be said that they would kill if neces-
sary. She was not afraid of dying so even the threat of
killing did not break her spirit. Of course that did not
mean she did not suffer the pain of endless tongue lash-
ings, ridicule, whippings, time spent in isolation. She suf-
fered. In spite of the suffering, her spirit grew.

Don't get me wrong. Suffering did not make her
strong. She was always a sickly fragile thing, over-
whelmed by fears, a creature of strange habits and
strange ways. She had nightmares, cried every day. No
wonder then they told her she was crazy, that she would
end up in a mental institution, that no one would visit
her there.

I have trouble sleeping. Nightmares ride me down. It's
been that way as long as I remember. The more they
punish me, the worse the nightmares. Past the age of
thirteen I can only think that dying is one way to make
the pain stop. I have no tolerance for physical pain. When
I begin to bleed regularly, I am in agony. I can hardly
work. I hate the fragility of the body.

When I leave home for college, I believe the nightmares will stop, that they are somehow connected to this
past I am leaving behind, but they continue. Before I left
home, I had begun to worry about myself because I kept
longing, even against my will, to die. As soon as I entered
college, I found my first psychiatrist. He was not at all
interested in my pain. He was more interested in the way
I saw him, in talking about his problems.

20

We meet when feminist movement is rocking the campus. My favorite professor is Diane Middlebrook, a sexy woman who thinks and writes and takes no prisoners. She is everything we—her students—want to be. She cares and nurtures our spirits. She is not just into our minds. In her poetry class she passes out one of my poems—with no name on it. Our discussion for the day has to do with gender and writing. We have to answer whether work by women is different from work by men. When we read the poem, no one can tell the gender of the writer.

Difference does not lie in gender I am thinking—but say nothing. If we are socialized properly the way we think may follow predetermined sexist norms but if indeed we are struggling to resist those notions from the day we are born, then the boundaries between male and female are blurred. Middlebrook, which is what we call her, makes us think. We come to her class excited. Most of the women who come to this class are in all the new "women's studies" classes. As usual they are all white. In these classes we rarely mention race. We are struggling to think deeply about the issues of women writing, about whether we need rooms of our own, stipends, about whether we can write and have husbands, lovers, children, whatever we want—the issue is creativity and writing. Her class excites and frightens.

It is as though Middlebrook takes all the issues we have been talking about since girlhood on inside her students and brings them out in the open. This end to silence is so nurturing to our spirits and at the same time, now that these secrets are no longer locked away, we have to confront more, make more difficult choices, we have to feel more pain. Our woman-only dances, our sleepovers, our consciousness-raising groups, our new "out" lesbian and bisexual love affairs, none of these marvelous things change the fact that if we want to be liberated women we have to make difficult choices. It's not just who we love but how we will love. It's not just claiming the space of writing, it's also about being clearer about what we write and who we write for. Most of us are not political girls. We've been the introverts, the hidden in the corner, sexually excited but reserved, smart girls wanting to nurture our minds. Now, all the freedom we dreamed of is being offered to us only we have to claim it—we have to struggle and demand—we have to resist. Naturally we are often confused.

We were antimarriage. I made it clear to mama that she could never hope that there would be any wedding bells for me. At sixteen I knew marriage was out of the question. Marriage as she lived it as I had seen it around me was all about possession. The only marriage that even remotely interested me was the one between Baba and Daddy Gus. Together forever, certainly more than sixty years by the time I was in college, they did not sleep in the same room. Their rooms clearly reflected the difference in their personalities. This intrigued me. And of course they went their separate ways. They were bound and not bound. They had their separate friendships, habits of being, and did not even eat together. But they were close and committed.

Daddy hated their relationship. He believed Baba, our grandmother, dominated Daddy Gus. He wasn't the only one who felt this way. I remember asking mama once if someone has to be dominated isn't it better then for the woman to dominate the man—that way the woman does not have to be the one who hurts, who bears the pain. At Stanford we are dreaming a world where there will be no need to worry about anyone getting hurt. We are dreaming a world of equals. At first Mack is not that into feminism. He thinks all the girls on campus who are into women's liberation are really lesbians—not that he minds—but he doesn't see anything for men to get excited about. Although we read the *SCUM Manifesto*, and some of us express rage at men, we are not that interested in men. We are passionate about our futures. It's

145

trying to work out who we are and what we long for and what fulfillment means to us that's the hard part of women's liberation. Later for thinking about men.

Those of us who are into men do know that we cannot be about the business of becoming more fully ourselves if we are still spending all our time trying to seduce men. Our focus has to shift. We look for men who can accept and support this shift in focus. As he courts and seduces me, he claims to be ready for women's liberation. And yet he seems to forget that tell-all, heart-to-heart talk I had with his previous partner. She was definitely the woman behind the man. That's the way he really likes it, she told me. Based on this conversation, I confront him with the big issues—housework, marriage, children. Only one of those three interests me and I want to know that it will be shared. We agree to share the housework, and that included cooking. He was one step ahead of me. I had never cooked anything. Living alone mostly I did not eat. I was too busy doing something else. When I tried to shy away from cooking he reminded me of the terms of our agreement and so I cooked.

The hardest thing for me was that I did not know how to drive. And worse that I feared driving. It was hard to be equal if I was always dependent on him to give me a ride. That's when we began to talk about in our groups and in our relationships the problem of equality. Should everything be the same. If men were already more privileged than women, a step ahead, then how could we start off as equals. This was the age of birth control and abortion rights. At least there we felt we had gained the rights to determine the future of our bodies. And then there was sexuality—those of us who continue to be with men find they are more than willing to cook, clean, and do their share but when it comes to sex—they still believe we are there to satisfy male desire. If we throw in some little desire of our own that simply makes their satisfaction more intense. How to make men see that our bodies belong to us and are not there to satisfy anyone's desire.

In our house it is a constant struggle. Every time he is sexually aroused he thinks his needs should be satisfied. I think that he must assume primary responsibility for the fulfillment of his desire—that I do not have to respond. Still words are not enough. There is not just the will to say no, but the strength to push bodies away, then the strength to bear the punishment that we have rejected them—silence, withdrawal, withholding of affection. None of the feminist books, none of our women's studies classes tells us how to cope with the move from inequality to equality. Does everything have to be the same for things to be equal.

I decide that the issue is not sameness, that equality cannot be measured this way. That we all have to map our journeys according to our own desires. If I hate taking out the garbage and don't want to, and he does not mind, then that can be his chore even though it has always been defined as the male chore (at least it was in our family). The point of course is that I must still know how to take out the garbage. And in our case I hate to do the shopping so he does. I love to clean so I do most (not all) of the cleaning. So we begin with equality in that we both have the skills to do the same chores, then we break them down according to desire making sure that everything balances out in the end.

All this is easier for us because we do not have children. In our groups women with children have the most problems in relationships with men. We have decided not to have children. He says he does not like children. I love children and want them in my life. Growing up I was made to feel that smart women make bad mothers. I know differently. As soon as I left home I let my love for children express itself whenever I was around them. Working with my ten two-year-old kids at the day-care center what I learned most was that children take time and energy. I was so tired when I came home from work, I decided not to have children not because I did not love them, or did not think I would be a good mother, but because I worry all the time about the issue of time and tiredness. Anyway I have plenty of time to think about whether or not to have children. He is more certain than I am that he never wants to have a child.

21

To be baptized in the name of the father, the son, and the holy ghost, to make one's vow to the lord and not turn back—this is the passion that calls me in childhood. Confined in my small spaces with no light I dream that I have found my true destiny—to be the bride of god, to be a contemplative. Church is one of the few public places where I feel that presence of magic. Baba says she went to church once and there was such hypocrisy there that she never went back. The real story was that she went for a while but the absence of truth did make her flee. And it is true she never went back.

They go to church every Sunday, and in midweek they go to prayer meeting, and sometimes they go back on Sunday for evening service. Religion inspires her. It is the place of hope—the seat of her belief that her life will be

*better someday, that none of her suffering will be in vain.
At church she enters a world of mystery and possibility—
there she learns about the mystical dimensions of Chris-
tian faith. To be mystical one has to fully embrace the
mysterious, the unknown.*

*The night she is baptized, they wear white. White
covers them. A sense of the sacred surfaces as children
who would otherwise be loudly talking together prepare
in silence to face symbolic ritual death. In a dark room lit
by candles they hear voices singing* Wade in the water,
children—god's gonna trouble the water. *There is the
night's mystery. In what way will the water be troubled.
Will the spirits in the water touch her with their grace.
Everyone trembles in the darkness. It is her turn to
be baptized in the name of the father, the son, and the
holy ghost.*

That night I was so full of longing. I believed I would be
made new by this immersion in blessed holy water. My
spirits I believed would be renewed. And they were. I left
the church thinking about the preacher saying I baptize
this my sister, thinking about a place of godliness where
men and women stand as equals, as sisters and brothers
in the body of Christ. That fascinates me. In my bed that
night I imagine the holy ghost coming to me, revealing
that this unknown unnamed force is the power of the
daughter, the mother, the sister. They are the shadows
that haunt in this church where only men are imagined.
John the Baptist his arms around Jesus the Christ is

pictured there. John the voice of one crying in the wilderness, John who comes to bear witness to the light, who testifies I am not worthy. He is the writer, the bringer of the word, the word that will be made flesh.

Religion offers me a way to understand the meaning of passion. The marks on his hands are a sign of love's suffering. The blood that we drink for the remission of sin. The bread that we break that is his body. This is the path I can follow that can lead to paradise, to that garden where I come alone to meet him. Here is the place for our collective passion. We sing: *I come to the garden alone, while the dew is still on the roses. And the voice I hear falling on my ear, the son of god discloses. And he walks with me, and he talks with me, and he tells me I am his own; and the joy we share as we tarry there, none other has ever known.* The root word of passion, *patior*— to suffer.

I suffer and through suffering my faith falters. When I pray for rescue no god comes. In the stillness of the night, as I lie in my girlhood, I am learning to question god even as I surrender to the passion. If nothing else I will die and be born again, die and resurrect. In resurrection of the body lies my hope for I have learned that *though worms destroy this body, yet in the flesh shall I see god.*

She moves closer to god through service. In her girlhood she learns that it is vital that she do for others, that she give, generously, selflessly. She makes her offerings on the altar of sacrifice where her all must be laid. Since

151

she has been given a sweet voice and a love of reading it is her task to read the scriptures to those who are infirm, who cannot read, whose eyes see poorly. And so she sits and reads for hours—reading aloud, explaining as best she can what the scriptures mean. To her it is all poetry.

When I come to college, it does not take me long to realize that the really hip people do not believe in god, that no one talks about religion except the boring born agains. My relationship to god is the most private union. I learn not to speak of it. Although in classes it is always I who can name a scriptural reference. I know the bible and am not ashamed of this knowing. In fact, it surprises me that everyone in my classes is so ignorant, mostly though they brag about being atheist. That's what is really cool—to not believe in the existence of god. I believe.

Daily I go the Stanford church, the ornate temple of god built in remembrance of the son that died. I love the stillness in the church. When I enter the sanctuary all the cares and hardships I feel daily fall away and there is for me here a place of peace. I come to the church to pray. Prayer is definitely not a hip gesture. To me prayer is as essential to life as breathing. To talk with god is to enter the place of mystery and possibility.

Mack finds my devotion to religion strange. I have moved away from the conventional church but I have kept in me the love of the inner life, the need to be one with the divine. I search for the meaning of religious life everywhere. I study Buddhism and Islamic mysticism. In town there is a Sufi meeting. I go there to dance in the circle of love. All that I am learning about the mystical dimensions of religious faith takes me back to the heart, to loving. To be with god is to love. *It is required and understood that a man be found faithful.* The ethics of being that govern my life are grounded in spiritual life.

He says he believes in higher powers but did not grow up going to church. *Oh! they went every now and then but not often.* And the last time he went as a child the preacher preached a sermon about the fires of hell, and all this stuff that scared him, and he never wanted to go back. He believes but he is not sure of what he believes. He does not know the bible.

I read my favorite passages to him. The Psalms that tell me to *delight in the Lord and he will give me the desires of the heart.* His real name means "gift from god." When we first met I felt indeed that he was my blessing come to rescue me from the well of loneliness I was falling into, from isolation and estrangement. I tell him that to be estranged from one's community is to sin. They were put here on earth to be together, to tarry together.

He is never present when I pray. And is always embarrassed when we are with family and he is asked to lead us in prayer. My relationship with god is my most private union. I have no need to share that moment with him or anyone else. I have no need to convert anyone to my way of thinking about life. We rarely speak of god. Sometimes I find a passage he is searching for to use as a reference for something he is writing.

Prayer is my refuge and my sanctuary. To talk with god is to return to a place in the heart where one is understood fully and deeply. To seek a place to pray is to find the place of stillness. Everyone leads such a life of busyness—that stillness is always lacking. No wonder then that prayer has no place. It is this need for a solitary place that enables me to leave spaces in my life open, to not overbook myself. Life is not something that should be always scheduled. And what calendar can contain one's relationship to the divine. I learn not to speak of these things.

She is there right at that moment when everyone is looking to Eastern thought and religion for revelation. Constantly seeking she reads everything, goes to this and that meeting, but she can never make a choice, never find that one faith and stick to it. When questioned about this she resolutely states that her faith is rooted in the experience of divine love not in organized religion but that too has its place. Buddhism and Islamic mysticism these are the two traditions that she studies the most, that move her away from the Christianity of her youth.

Shortly before I came to live with Mack I thought again about the contemplative religious life—that maybe the monastery is for me. More and more I think that Zen Buddhism is the path I most want to follow. I meet a Buddhist monk at Gary Snyder's place in the mountains. We talk about stillness, following the path with heart. Just to be in her presence is to feel calm and whole again as though the broken bits and pieces of the heart are put together again. Even though I am often alone in life, I think too much about the things of this world and this thinking makes me feel I am not ready for a spiritual path. But I go on seeking.

He does not take her religious seeking seriously. Not even when she travels with him to North Africa in search of a teacher. Already she has dragged him into the Bodhi Tree, into the world of Swami Satchidananda and her latest passion Bhagwan Shree Rajneesh. And even when she speaks of going to India to continue her search he thinks it's all just fantasy. He does not identify because there is no desire in him to be a seeker on the path, no such longing. He has found his gods and they are all roaming around the world having fun.

Despite his lack of interest in the subject, Mack turns me on to the world of the Buddhist teacher Trungpa. That's because Naropa is also a place where poetry is celebrated. The poets we know spend lots of time telling us about the wild Mr. Trungpa and his wicked ways. Mack is interested. This a way to quest for the divine that he can understand, hedonistic play. I am not sure I am ready to meet, come anywhere near the real Trungpa. I would rather pore over the texts of *Cutting Through Spiritual Materialism.*

Even though I know books are not enough, do not even come close to the realm of spiritual experience, will definitely not be the meditation that leads me to nirvana,

I am still reading and searching. There is still so much for me to understand before I can make a choice, choose a path. And I am not sure what will happen if Mack does not wish to come on that path with me.

She goes to all those different groups. She is always the only black person in sight. They welcome her but always remind her that in their eyes she is exotic—they want to know what brought her to Buddhism and what kindled her interest in Islamic mysticism—even as they take their interest to be natural, normal. She finds that she dislikes with passion most of the white Americans who participate in the various groups. They are so arrogant and presumptuous, never questioning their own relationship to the cultures and traditions they are turning to. She tries not to judge but even so she has to admit her profound annoyance. That feeling intensifies when folks talk about how they do not need to do anything about racism because we have chosen our race, our class. It fascinates her that so many privileged white people are into Buddhism and the like. And yet she never encounters them in her walks toward the divine.

Finally, I decide that there is no path I can travel on except the path of love. I decide that it is fine to travel alone. I have found this incredible book, conversations between Vietnamese Buddhist monk Thich Nhat Hanh and activist Daniel Berrigan. In that book I learn from the Buddhist monk to understand the meaning of aloneness and to not fear it. He says that "when you decide to be yourself you will be alone." And while he talks about the necessity of community, he describes communities that are always changing. At last I have a moment of clarity I can cling to. I meditate. I find the path of stillness even though I do not know which tradition calls me. I know only that I am called to love. That to love is to serve.

It seems that this missionary nonsense was bred into her early on from church. It ain't all nonsense but she takes it too far. Folks be pretending that they need money and stuff and she be trying to give and they just be lying a lot of the time. Sometimes after folks get what they want out of her that's it; they don't come around anymore. He understands the evil in people more than she does. That's why she feels safe with him. Only she might be safer if she thought a little harder about why it is he understands the evil more.

It's funny, in the beginning he loved all that innocence in her. That she was willing to push past a lot to try to find the jewel inside everyone. But then it just started to get on his nerves. He just began to feel like why not go somewhere else if you want to be a missionary. At least she did not try to talk much to him about all that religious stuff. He was into the poetry. Reading Rumi and the like. But that was enough mystery for him. Luckily, when they went to the desert in North Africa they never found the teacher she was looking for so he did not have to deal with that disappointment. He was sure it was disappointment. She just expected too much from life, too much from humans.

Godliness—that is what I thought about. How do we create that in our daily lives. Since I was a girl I was always taught that one should serve and give without calling attention to oneself or the gift. Sometimes though it seems like I am living two separate lives. At school where everyone thinks I am difficult and demanding. And this other life where I am devoted to the practice of humility.

One way I cope with these two identities is to have different names. As a writer I use the name bell hooks. This is the name of my mother's mother's mother—my great mother. Old folks used to always address me as you must be kin to bell hooks, look like her and talk like her. Talking like her meant that I spoke my mind—clearly and decisively. Two names will help me to practice detachment—remind me always that I am not my writing always something more. And that it is useful not to be too identified with the ego.

There is this ongoing conflict between my involvement in academic life, which seems to place so much emphasis on the ego, and my commitment to spiritual life. Even striving to be a writer demands more of a public self than I want to be. The contemplative life is so much the life I long for—the space I need to write in. A space of refuge and quiet and stillness. I find it hard to read my work at poetry readings. I try though. Yet it does not satisfy me. And only Mack knows how much I fear being in a crowd. We both know the days of sitting in one's room like Emily Dickinson and writing through the dead still silence into life is over. I have to learn to cope better with being a public person. Mack knows more and helps me. Even he does not understand how much I feel called to a life of stillness.

How can he understand when I keep these thoughts to myself. Not always to myself. I talk about everything in my prayers. And I keep a journal. In a fit of rage I burned years of journal writing—stuff from my childhood, my days at Stanford. This is an action I regret because there is so much I can't remember. Layers of memories like paint cover one another and it is hard to know what is underneath, what really happened. Mack stands between me and the world. I have difficulty knowing when to say no—how not to get involved with people, how not to serve. He builds a wall. His manner is a No Trespassing sign.

She should be learning how to set boundaries with people. But she doesn't. He sets all the boundaries. She has a room of her own—she goes there only after the needs of the relationship are met or because he is spending all the time in his study. She is really learning how to be alone with herself as a writer. She is used to being alone for prayer and contemplation, but is she really able to claim the space of solitude for work.

159

．　．　．

I contemplate my work. I pray for divine guidance. It comes between me and Mack that I am turning from poetry to writing critical essays, on subjects that are more political. He feels I am abandoning the aesthetics of the artist life for the mundane realm of social theory. I am trying to invent a world that can sustain me as a writer, as a woman dedicated to the life of the mind. I want to remain a seeker on the path.

22

Although we live in the City of Angels, there is no protection anywhere. Our guardians cannot be seen. Here more than anyplace else we see the world differently. I am always sad. The therapist wants to give me drugs. I meditate. It helps. But nothing makes the sadness go away. I lose interest in so much sex. It's always been the bond between us, sex and writing. He is also writing. Not poetry but work for tenure. He ignores me until he wants to have sex. I wander around the streets. It takes a while for me to understand that men in cars think I am a prostitute. To be a young black woman taking a long slow walk on a sunny day on a busy street in Los Angeles is to be a streetwalker. I stop walking.

We talk more now about being involved with other people. He has old girlfriends. From the first moment we met he would tell everything about his old flames, who sucked the best dick and how, whose breasts were perfect, who had good pussy, who liked doing it from behind or being fucked in the ass. I listen and absorb. He is so into sex. And I am still so shy. Before him I only had two other partners; the sex was nothing to talk about.

These days life revolves for him around work and sex. He ignores me. I pursue one of my other passions—fashion. Since I don't have much money (and no credit—I've messed up my credit by buying conservative clothes for jobs I searched for and did not get, for jobs I got and left—anyhow it wasn't worth it). I've always been one of those shoppers who finds the goodies in secondhand stores. Our flat is beautiful and everything in it I have found at the cheap shops, at garage sales. Sometimes I make a little money buying for other people and decorating their places. I have a good eye for placing things. Everywhere we live is beautiful. I am always getting rid of things, changing space, making it new. He is not interested in these changes. Only two things in his life matter right now, work and sex. He ignores me.

When we first moved here he introduced me to one of those women, Ann. Although he had always talked about her beauty and sexiness I found her downright plain and rude. The three of us went out to eat and she ignored me completely, flirting with him as though I was not present. That did not bother me. But then we begin to discuss race. And she says, looking directly at me, *that she can't stand those black people who go on and on talking about being black* and I know when I am being insulted. It's one thing to invite me out to dinner (this was her idea) and ignore me, quite another to insult me and my race so I defend my honor. I tell her loudly so everyone can hear *Look, bitch, I don't play this shit. Don't invite me out to dinner to insult me. I will slap you across that room.* And just as I am raising my hand to do just that she runs out. I look directly at him, daring him to run after her. Even though he stays, of course I get a lecture about controlling myself. I see it as a matter of not letting white folks disrespect you, play you like you are stupid, as in I was too stupid to know that girlfriend was saying she did not like black people like me. He did not stand by me although he did not go running out to comfort Miss Ann. And even when I try to explain that people can speak quietly and nicely and still be vicious and mean, he still thinks I am the one who has a problem. Let's not forget though, he needs to be adored and admired. I left out that she was emphasizing how much she liked the way he deals with issues like race. No comment. Well open relationship or not he will have to rhapsodize about this tired white girl pussy to somebody else, about the virtues of her dick-sucking mouth. I, mind you, do not have the perfect dick-sucking mouth.

She was not against interracial dating. Her first lover was a white man and she had been with other white men. To her the issue was one not of race but racism. She was never turned on by any white man that she could see clearly was into a "black thing." Any man she slept with was someone whose heart she had looked into and liked what she saw. In the beginning it was hard for her, a southern black girl, to think about having sex with someone white. You couldn't grow up in the apartheid south and not know that the average white man looked at black women as sexual savages, wild things, bush mamas; mammy, whore, or prostitute, take your pick; that's the way it was. No wonder most black women felt they had to stay away from white men. She would have loved to have had black men with good hearts standing in line, longing to be close to her. When she was tired of being a virgin, she wanted to have sex someone kind and gentle, someone who would be understanding, someone she did not have to love. When that person came along she did not think twice about the question of color.

Mack is one of the few black men I've met who is not disturbed by the fact that I have had sex with white men and no doubt will have some more sex with white men before the day is done. Before moving in with him I use to hang out with the street black men who came on campus to sell their wares, with some of the Muslim brothers. They would rant and rave about a sister who would do it with a white man. That sister was a traitor to the race. Of course the brother doing it with a white woman was not betraying the race in their eyes, he was just getting some pussy. Pussy had no power, no color, but dick now that was tied to meaningful manhood, to notions of privilege and choice and power. Manhood was manhood precisely because it could not be told what to do. It could not be shaped and formed like clay. But pussy was pussy; it had no color and no allegiance. I listened to these raps but I always do what I want to—fuck whomever I want to fuck just like the boys do.

That does not mean that I sleep around. I am sure Mack would have more of an attitude about being with me if I had just done it with everybody. Though he's not the judgmental type when it comes to desire and that's one of the things I really like about him. From the beginning I tell him I see myself as bisexual and that does not bother him either. He probably has some fantasy of him and me in bed with some girl of my choice—but I don't think so. Clearly, we are not attracted to the same type of girl. Standing in a long registration line at school I pass the time checking out people in the line. I stare intently at a woman reading a book by Lorca. I am totally impressed that someone in this line is reading poetry. She glances up now and then and smiles. She has an oddly attractive look, somewhat androgynous like Patti Smith. We strike up a conversation and I learn that she is from Spain, that she is Catalan, a graduate student like myself, and she is married to Harry, a nice Jewish boy, even though she was raised Catholic. We admire each other's clothes and plan to get together which we do to listen to music, to eat.

Maria Rosa lives at Venice Beach in one of those tiny apartments with lots of interesting rooms where you can never find a parking place. It's far from where we live in

Hollywood and my little red car is always breaking down but I come to visit, to eat, to talk poetry, to listen to music. She raves all the time about her brother who is becoming a psychiatrist like her father. At times we tease her that she is in love with her brother. At times Mack teases me that I am in love with Maria Rosa.

Between us it is not so much the issue of falling in love as it is finding another eccentric soul in this world who does not find you and your ways strange. My friends are foreign students who do not find me or my ways strange. They say to me all the time *you don't seem very un-American*. I always say I'm a Kentuckian—region always rather than nation. The south I always say is different, not like New York, not like Los Angeles, different. When they want to know different how I tell them time is slower, kindness is valued, and so is conversation. Of course even as I say this I know that the south of my childhood is changing, that the good differences (of course I have to speak the ways the south is a cruel place) are slowly being washed away by the longing to no longer stand in the shadow of the north—so the south in some places is becoming in many ways a cheaper version of the north.

When Maria's brother comes he too has a strange look, one that charms me especially when he smiles. The way he says his English is just too delightful for words. Like Mack he loves music. They talk music endlessly playing this and that cut. I cook lots and we all hang out except for Mack who continues to work, who joins us sometimes.

One Friday night they plan a party in Venice and we go. I rarely drink but I'm having sangria tonight like everybody. Alcohol makes me sad. Hard liquor makes me crazy. No thanks.

The party has so much good food. It disappears. I bring Indian food—that's the cuisine I cook the most. For vegetarians it's the most exciting stuff. Eggplant and okra curries are my specialities. And a chicken korma I no longer eat but love to make. Jöan, Maria Rosa's brother, enchants me. He is her in boy body but different from her in his ideas and beliefs. He and I are more alike. Brazilian music is playing in the background. He is holding me close and whispering silly things in my ear and I can feel the heat of our bodies. It makes me wet all over like steam.

When the dancing is done, I sit with Mack on the crowded couch and whisper to him: *I think you should be the first to know. I am falling in love with that man across the room.* He laughs at me. I point him out. Maria's brother. Mack says he smells bad. It's my time to laugh. I like the way he smells. Before the night is done I declare the need to spend more time with this Catalan man, lover of music, healer of mind and heart, a man with what Mack calls a dick-sucking mouth. Oh well, it's a mouth I like.

We form the perfect triangle: me, Maria Rosa, Jöan. Everyone is happy that we spend so much time together. Mack is glad that I no longer pester him to stop work. I feel that my sadness is lifting. Maria Rosa is sometimes sad too, and cries in my arms, cries unexpectedly. We love to go to the sea together, the three of us. We sing songs, play, and pretend we are little children again who have no cares in the world.

In Maria Rosa's house Jöan sleeps in a little room off from the kitchen. There is a record player by the bed. We listen to Stevie Wonder. We make love on this narrow bed listening to Stevie Wonder and telling each other the stories of our lives. Everyone has an opinion about our relationship. Mostly that they feel sorry for Mack. They don't know about his love affairs with other women. Mack is always secretive. He always appears one way and acts another. He likes his public image to be untarnished—intact. It helps everyone to see me as the dominating woman who flaunts her love for another man, wounding Mack. Everyone feels for him.

I feel that it is time for him to be the one who is patient in this "open" relationship. Since he likes sex more than I do, openness has always been more inviting to him. He fucks other people. I stay home. Now it's different. I am not just sleeping with another man. I am saying I love this funky Catalan man even though this love is only for a time and has no future. Jöan has a long-time girlfriend he plans to marry.

Sex with Jöan is not as good as sex with Mack. But I am not here for the sex. Like me Jöan believes in the healing of broken hearts. Mack thinks all forms of therapy are weakness. Jöan and I talk and talk about childhood. Mack never likes to do anything silly. Jöan and I play. We sing and dance a lot. We both like to see what is in each other's hearts and the hearts of other people.

Even though I have chosen to be a writer the other profession that always fascinated me is psychoanalysis. Jöan and I talk endlessly about the meaning of therapy in modern life. We talk about his father the famous psychiatrist (doctor to Miró and other famous artists), about the way Jöan does not want to become his father, about the process of his rebellion. We talk about white men and black women. We talk about the fact that sex is important but not everything. We talk about love.

Mack says very little about me and Jöan. Our sex life continues as usual. The three of us hang out together, go to movies, go to concerts. He and Jöan still talk music. They never talk about us. There is no real us. Jöan plans to marry his long-term girlfriend. Mack has no interest in me and Jöan until everyone else begins to talk. One night we go to a party at their place with the usual crowd. I am sometimes with Mack and sometimes with Jöan. Everyone looks.

Mack is ready to go home sooner than I am. I tell him to go and I will come later or not at all. Upset, he tells me to come with him. I insist on staying even though I have no way to get home. I tell him if need be I will stay the night. Pissed off he walks out. I am torn between keeping the peace at home and longing to stay with Jöan who just stands silently by waiting. He does not try to influence the outcome.

Mack comes back, rings the bell, and yells for me to

come down. I refuse. I don't want to be yelled at. The yelling becomes pleading. I still refuse to come. My daring to spend the night with Jöan when Mack wants me to come home is the gesture I make that turns everyone in our set against me, even Maria Rosa. Suddenly, everyone sees Mack as the victim of a castrating bitch. Everyone is on my case. They tell me how I am wounding his masculinity. So much for free love, open relationships, feminism, and the like. I am public enemy number one. Mack tells me that this open relationship stuff is not working. He wants to change the way we are doing things. He asks me to stop seeing Jöan. I refuse. We talk about the ways our relationship is in trouble.

So much of the pleasure of being with Jöan is changed by everyone's rage at me. I am more than struck at the way behavior seen as bad on a woman's part is deemed worthy of everyone punishing her even though male behavior that is hurtful to women goes unnoticed. My refusal to admit that I have done anything wrong enrages everyone more. No one cares to hear about the agreements Mack and I have had—the ways he does not keep those agreements. Me, I keep our agreements.

He has not stopped seeing any woman because her presence in his life threatens me. I have not asked him to. Granted he does not say that he loves someone else. I am in love with Jöan. Even though I do not dream of making a life with him. I would never want to live in Spain and he would never want to live here. I do not speak his language. I tell him always: *I think you do not really know another person if you cannot speak their language. And so there are limits to the way we know each other.*

The love I feel for Jöan threatens my life with Mack and makes me see him and the ways we are together in a new way. It's hard though cause I know that he and I are just at different places in our lives. He's worried sick about tenure even though he does not share those worries with me. I am disillusioned with academic life and need a break. It's understanding our different longings and needs right now that created the space in me to long for someone else. Even though I am the one who insists on a politics of openness, I am not the one who consistently longs for other people. My bonding with Jöan is full of light and helps me chase the shadows away.

23

She has a thing about houses, a real obsession, always had, even when she was a real little girl. Then it was doll-houses. There was this preacher's wife who went to her home church (that's the church you were baptized in) who was a collector of dollhouses. If girls were really good they got to take a trip to her house and play with this huge dollhouse.

Some things about childhood I remember so vividly. The place we lived in when I was a child had concrete floors. I remember the grayness of those floors, slate gray—the coldness against naked feet. I remember the hurt from falling out of bed—onto cold concrete—the blood against the gray. The coldness of the house touches me sometimes and I can hardly bear it. Memories are like that. They haunt me as though there is no real life just the realness of the memories. Wood-frame houses filled with passion and pain. Shacks across town where pleasure and danger lurk.

She was that kinda person you know. One of those folks who just stood in front of houses that enchanted her, staring. They were always small wood-frame places, nothing but firetraps—that's what Baba used to say. That's why she loved them. They were delicate, tender, easy to be broken. If you threw an object at somebody in one of those walls it left its mark. If you pressed neatly greased hair against those walls a print was left—a shadow of a body here and there, body that left its trace. Aretha Franklin, Otis Redding, and all the oldies but goodies were the music you heard coming out of those houses. She had found love in those shacks, the unconditional love of her Big Mama. She wanted to live in one when she grew up, live in a shack and paint it yellow.

I had such a passion for houses, shacks mostly. Really it was any structure, space. I don't know why I never dreamed of being an architect then. Not even when I designed the house of my dreams in Mr. Harold's art class—not the way he spelled his name. It was the way the black folks spelled it. We were all surprised when we looked in the yearbook and saw how the white folks did it. Growing up we thought they did not have our love of words and language. We knew language could dance, cry, do just about anything. When I designed that house for

173

Mr. Harold, I never thought how much I was telling him about myself, about that girl who cried herself to sleep at night in pink attic rooms she shared with other girls who did not know enough about the way love could change the look and feel of a place. I knew this as a girl, shacks did not have concrete floors. I wanted a world of wood underneath my feet. Gleaming wood that the sun could heat, that could be cool in winter but always capable of being warmed up. Concrete was never warm enough.

I dreamed about houses all the time, the one I would make and build for myself. A small wood-frame place with cot-sized beds. It was my desire to sleep alone, to keep a bed to myself. I needed to know that there were places inside and outside myself no one could enter, private places. Growing up all I had for a long time was my bed.

When I met him he lived in a little house, just like the ones I was always standing in front of, holding my longing for shelter and sanctuary. Houses I used to go to in the night and plead with to take me, to give me shelter. The house I lived in was a huge rambling Victorian, turned into little apartments. It reminded me of a railroad shack, everything moving straight back in a line. Houses where you could have no fear, nothing could be hidden from you, everything was right there in your face and there was nothing to fear—nothing.

Once she saw his house, it was only a matter of time before she would seek to live there. It did not even bother

174

her that the other woman had left her things. She liked the touch and feel of the other woman's presence. It was as though it reminded her of the way things were always fluid, always running into one another. It reminds her of the ways you could not possess things or people for long. She was not into possession. The houses she had grown up knowing were all places where folks hungered to possess things so tightly, they choked them to death.

It was in that house on First Street, the one with the porch they loved, that she would feel those invisible hands around her neck choking the life out of her and everything else. Those hands belonged to somebody who knew their father. They were not his hands, she was sure of it. They were strange hands that held them tightly bound by lies and secrets and jealousies as monstrous as any nightmares. She would lie awake in those pink attic rooms and try to pry those fingers loose. They were a dead person's hands, she knew it. A jealous dead person who did not want anybody to have their fair share of love.

That's the kinda girl she was, always creating a story to take her mind off the pain. Her daddy's jealousy had an ice cold grip on everything. That's what happens when an old hound dog marries a young pretty wife. Even in his sleep he dreams that someone is desiring to take her as he has taken her again and again, so he torments her. That's the secret in this house—torment.

Moving frightened me. When we first left the hill, where I had spent my early childhood, to move down the road to First Street, I grieved. It had taken me all my life to come

175

to terms with concrete, with the round gray tubs we bathed in—with the wildness of the outdoors around us. I did not want to move into pink attic rooms in a world that strange. It did not take long for that grief to turn into a long slow torment that would last long after the house on the hill had been torn down to make room for fancy red-brick projects. And we were all there in that large wood-frame house on First Street. Mr. Porter's house. He had owned and lived there forever. We never knew him but we talked about him and to him all the time. I used to think he could explain everything about this house, about why everything in it hurt so much.

I lived in torment in that house. It started long before that day daddy came home and threatened to kill mama because he believed she was sleeping with another man, long before he slapped her face while she sat on the couch, silent as blood trickled down her mouth. That moment just intensified the torment I felt. He made her pack her things that night, and leave just like that. She called one of her brothers to come and get her. I thought he would come and tell daddy not to hurt his sister, not to touch her ever again in this way. Yet he greeted daddy with the same voice he had always used. He said nothing as he packed mama's things in the car. I was one of those things.

His rage was always a killing rage. He had unleashed it that night in a way that could not be stopped. She was the child that watched. The pain that night seemed to make some sense of her torment. She was more than willing to

176

leave that house when he turned to her mama's posses-
sions and yelled Take that one with you. She was just that
then, another one of her mama's possessions like a
favorite lamp, the little jars on her vanity, the boxes of
handkerchiefs, small things that could be packed away.
Leaving that house in the middle of the night was fine
with her. She had never wanted to live there.

We went that night to mama's childhood home. Her old
room was filled with somebody else's things. Everybody
grown knew that mama would not stay at Twelve Hundred Broad Street long. I did not know that. I never
wanted to go back to that other house. I did not even care
about the brother and sisters left sleeping on First Street.
We went back though. And I contined to live with the
torment.

Shacks don't have upstairs. That's why she loved them so.
Her folks never fought. That's why she took it so hard
when that night came. His yelling and reaching for his
gun, his talk of killing, his angry punishing hands—it was
too much for her, the sound of her mama weeping. She
would hear it every day. Those sounds were like heart-
beats at the center of the torment. She could never be
peaceful in a two-story house.

The place he lived in was almost a shack. I loved its little
rooms, filled with her things. I even loved the three black
cats she had left there. They were part of her presence—
a constant reminder not to possess things, to let them

177

come and go. I was always ready to welcome her back—
to make room. She was never the other woman to me but
someone he had lived with, still cared for, someone I had
connected with—intensely. It is me who wears her coat
in winter, who laid it lovingly in the trunk when he went
to take her things. She had moved to the City of Angels
where she could mourn and try to forget. We never saw
her again but we remembered her ways, her presence
cherishing the small things she had left behind.

We left that house. It was hard to find another one.
The search for hardwood floors, windows, places that
would be filled with light. Every place we lived in
together was beautiful. I needed that. I needed home to
be a sanctuary, a place where I could hide away. He was
totally laid-back about where we lived. He had grown up
living in apartments. I had grown up in houses and
everyone I knew lived in houses. There were no projects
then not on the black side of town; they would come later
when I was already living.

*She was more than just "into" houses. Living space and
the arrangement of every object in that space was an
obsession with her. It would have driven anyone crazy
had they not been indifferent. He was not indifferent just
willing to see it as a female thing and let it go. He gave in
to her on that one thing—finding places and arranging
them. Even when she wanted to buy a house even though
she did not have a "real" job, he was willing to look, so
sure they would never be able to find anything.*

178

I hated renting from white landlords. The contempt and fear they showed when they saw black people coming to look at their places was one of the ways I saw through the myth of there being no racial prejudice in housing. For everyone in the world it seemed, land, housing, was always the boundary keeping everyone in place. To cross the boundary one had to pay the price.

She wanted a home in a world where she could forget about racist white people altogether. In the midst of racial apartheid growing up, that is what they had found a way to forget. She found them a house to buy and ways to buy it. He was the one though who was able to get a low-interest loan through his job. By then there was already inside them, in their relationship, a level of torment. She had tried to pretend it was not there by constantly moving, rearranging space. Often he came home from work and found she had sold the furniture, given things away that he was comfortable with. He thought she was mad. He tried to stop her. Rage stopped her— killing rage.

We moved so much, practically every year. I was always searching for the perfect space, the space where I would no longer feel the torment. I had never really been free of it. I thought beauty could calm me. I thought quiet could make stillness possible. We were constantly moving because I could not bear to the hear the sound of other people. I felt invaded by those sounds as if they were taking me over and leaving me no place where I could stake a claim, where I could settle.

She was always searching for a place where there would be peace. He did not understand her search and she did not either. She did not know why things bothered her so, other people's sounds. She thought it was because she was used to houses and land and not having to hear the neighborhoods. She loved fences, had grown up with them closing off space. She never connected it to unreconciled childhood fear and pain—never.

Mack started telling her she was crazy. She did not seem to notice. She did not even seem to understand that it was this deep-seated fear of being crazy that was part of the torment. In her mind she really believed it was all about a love for space, a longing to change things. She could not even see how every house they had lived in was like a prison. He controlled everything, all the comings and goings. He let her control one thing—the arrangement of objects in space. She was always a bird in a cage and she did not even know it. Being closed in was so natural to her, it was more real than anything wide open.

I loved tiny rooms, spaces where I could close myself in. The shacks I loved were full of small rooms. Growing up I had always found some small tight space to shut myself away. I could hide from the pain and the torment. I could feel the sweetest most private peace. That's what I always thought I was searching for in those spaces, the sweetest most private peace. Everywhere we lived, he and I sought private space to write. I never want to think or work in the same room with someone else. I need to be alone with language.

Everyone would come to our spaces and try to make much of the fact that the feminist woman had the small room and that he had the large wide open studies, full of books. I hated to be surrounded by books. I was only ever interested in the book I was reading at the time. When we would tell them that I always chose the smaller place, they continued to see it as an act of willful subordination and not the fulfillment of my desire, to be closed in, confined.

She had seen herself as a prisoner in childhood. One of the primary ways they punished her was to put her in confined space, usually dark, usually windowless. Her hatred of confinement changed when she found a space to rest, a space where the torment would cease. When they discovered she found herself there in the aloneness, the quiet, they stopped sending her away. When she asked permission to go into the small dark room that had been given her when her older brother left home, the answer was usually no.

I was sure that if we just found the right place, we would be at peace. My search for it was long and ruthless. I was

181

willing to do anything to find the right object, to make the space be everything we needed. Although he seemed to like the spaces in the end, he hated the way I was driven, the way I tried to drive him, to make him enter this longing.

When they were finally ready to look for a house they would buy, the relationship was already falling apart. She believed the house would bring them closer together. His rage was unrelenting during the time they searched for the house, during the early months. He ranted and raved about the madness of someone who did not have a "real" job wanting to buy a house, someone who had bad credit, someone who could not even qualify for a loan to buy a car. She sold her car to get money for the down payment. He always managed to forget the clever strategies she used, the way she saved and managed so that they could do things. He was so much like her father and she had never seen it. She began to see it though when she found the perfect house. Her passion was stronger than his rage.

I found the perfect house. The living room was nine feet by twenty-seven feet. It looked like a long hallway. The floors were wide-planked soft wood. It reminded me of a shop. Everything was so narrow. It had a red door. There was a room downstairs for his study and a room upstairs for mine. The upstairs was atticlike, with lots of slanted windows, and places where no tall person could stand upright. There was a bathroom upstairs and downstairs, a

182

wonderful brand-new kitchen, and even a small service porch. It had so many windows, so much light. I fell in love with this house and knew it would be ours. It was my heart's desire. I thought that the fulfillment of desire would ease the torment.

She suffered in the new house. She was so passionate about this house that he matched that love with rage. He humiliated her there, time and time again. He terrorized her there, made her come to hate living there. It was as though this house was a rival threatening his hold over her, threatening to be a space of confinement that would close even him out. He hated her passion for that house. She loved it. It was her first real home.

24

Dark chocolate is my favorite. I could eat it for days. Mixtures of salty and sweet intrigue me. As a kid I liked to eat salty potato chips and dark chocolate at the same time. I am remembering this now because life with Mack has become pretty bittersweet. Lately he's easily annoyed. Now it's because we are thinking of moving again.

The months before that it was because he got sexually involved with the woman we met at the poetry reading. As in every case of openness in our relationship we talk about it first. I share my sense that our own bonding is too fragile right now to handle this. That I think we should not get involved. Even though her husband is into me I am not interested. I am concerned about what's happening between Mack and myself. Without my agreement and my knowledge they have sex. He tells me afterwards. I don't want to deal with this—not his fucking someone else. I've always had to deal with that. Even when he wasn't fucking somebody else he was always naming his desire for somebody else. There's not been even a week in this relationship of more than ten years that I have not had to hear about the desirability of someone else.

At first she enjoyed his open expression of interest in other women. She believed anything could be coped with and accepted if it was faced honestly and openly. Well "honest" is the key word. He was never that honest. She just didn't see. Maybe it was because he would disclose things in bits and pieces and for him she thought that was good. She didn't expect everybody to be like her, to want to face things up-front. She understood their differences. Mostly though she was too understanding.

I always really wanted to be a psychoanalyst. And it's true I always turn everything, every relationship into a case. Even my relationship with myself. Cause that's how I survived childhood—working things out, trying to understand why things happened the way they did. Seeing mom and dad as people too and not just my parents helped. It took me a long time to work everything out but it made life sane. Understanding gave me something to hold on to. Funny, I know how to survive better in the world of my family than I do in the world outside it. Outside there is so much I don't understand.

She never lies. That's part of her problem. She does not understand that people don't want to hear the truth.

That's what one of them big white professors told her. He called her right on into that office and told her: Your problem is you want to tell the truth, nobody wants to hear the truth. Mack loved this. Cause he'd been trying to tell her the same thing for years.

Lies make me feel insane. They give me that sensation that I have just when an earthquake is beginning and then when it happens. At first you don't know what the fuck is going on and then suddenly it hits and you know and you still don't know what to do. So you just stand there while the whole fucking world around you is shaking and falling apart. I'm tired of discussing this shit with Mack. I just tell him: Look, if you keep lying to me I'm going to leave. When he's angry he mocks this idea— that "Miss I-Am-So-Committed-to-This-Relationship is ever going to leave."

She should have known she was in serious trouble when he began to mock her, telling her stuff like even if some-body better came along she would still stay with him cause she was so "into" commitment. She was. Inside she agreed. Commitment was about process, working stuff out and staying around to do just that. After all he was talking to the girl who had based her vision of love and life on the lives of two old country black people who had been married to one another for more than seventy years, and two white men who were somewhere in between, and even her parents who were not that happy and who she

186

thought might come alive if they got away from one another had been together forever. So she did not think much about leaving. She just always thought about working things out.

Mack hit me today. We were in the bathroom talking about moving, talking about whether he would take the job in Santa Cruz and whether or not we would leave Los Angeles. He was raising his voice. I can't remember what he was saying. I said something back and he turned and slapped me. It happened so fast. I can't even remember what the point was. I am shocked. Dad was the last person to slap my face. I don't hesitate to tell him Don't even try to say that you are sorry.

They are moving again. And she can't even see that in his mind she is the problem. He scapegoats her. If he has a problem at work and she is nowhere in sight, he finds ways to trace it back to her. When another black professor writes a negative letter for his tenure he screams and rages at her. She stands for everything black that has ever hurt him—ever. And Miss Psychoanalysis, she understands this too. It's when they start looking for a house to buy and this crazy white guy whose house is for sale threatens them on the street and starts calling them niggers and Mack does not respond except to heap rage at her—that's how he scapegoats her, telling her that if she did not want a house so bad they would not know this crazy white man.

187

They fight so much about this house that it's hard to believe that she still wants to go through with it. It's like she thinks that once they are settled everything will be fine, that everything will work out. When in a fit of rage, he destroys the expensive color television she bought secondhand from a visiting professor, she faces that their relationship is in serious trouble. They start off talking and suddenly Mack explodes.

The more Mack screams and rages, the calmer and more rational I get. That's because I can't stand screaming. Inside I'm just falling apart. I just want to plead with him to stop. But I've tried that. It makes everything worse. I can't believe that after a life together of more than ten years where we have never had fights, everything is suddenly so out of control. I think we need to talk to somebody. Mack refuses.

Last week when they were arguing yet again about money, school, the house, he took all the phones and hid them. She sees that this shit is serious. She is frightened but she thinks they can work it out. Then there is the day they are headed to the city fighting all the way. And on the way back, they were rushing back to go to a Joan Armatrading concert, they were fighting again. She was saying that she thinks he has all the issues from the past, about his mother and his father's alcoholism and his father's abandonment and all that and he should talk with someone. Only he is telling her to shut the fuck up.

Driving down the highway in a rage over eighty miles an hour he is screaming at her and telling her he is going to beat the shit out of her if she does not shut up. She cannot see it coming—just like she never saw it coming in childhood. And suddenly he makes a fist, throws back his hand with such force it smashes her glasses, even though he hits her repeatedly in the mouth. Blood splatters everywhere. He smiles and says, I see you've shut up now. What she remembers clearly is not what they were talking about but that all the other people in the cars next to them are watching. She wonders what she would do if she was one of those people.

When we get home, I wash my face. He leaves to go to the concert. I am in such pain. I try to find a doctor but it's late on a Saturday night. He's broken my tooth. When he comes home from the concert he talks to me like nothing has happened and tells me that he's leaving to go to Los Angeles to spend the weekend with his mother. I call her and tell her to talk to him, to tell him he needs to see somebody. She tells me: She can't respect a woman who will stay with a man who hits her. For some reason this makes me laugh because I am suddenly remembering myself at childhood being hit and dreaming of leaving.

That's what she has always believed you know. That if a man ever hit she would leave right that minute and not look back. And now it's happening and she's not leaving

*and she can't go forward—something in her has stopped.
Like when you put the pause button on the tape recorder
and you forget and you try to make the tape move forward but it won't. She is sitting on the steps on a Sunday
afternoon, looking at herself in the mirror, seeing her
mother's face there—with no lights in her eyes. She can't
see the future. She still thinks they can get through this,
they can work it out. She says therapy or she's leaving.
They see a therapist.*

There is not one black therapist here so we see someone
white. I don't think it has to be a problem. It depends on
the therapist and this woman is Jewish and comes well
recommended. When we go to see her, she just listens to
us talk about why we came. Without asking any questions
she says: You two are poison for each other and need to
get away from each other right now. Mack turns to me
with such a look of satisfaction. At last we have the
answer from the oracle I wanted us to go and see. When
we walk out he is pleased. I am enraged at her violation of
us—and see this as a racist assault—since I know white
couples who see her for similar reasons and they've not
had this experience.

I am so upset that Mack is pleased and in no way
critical of the experience we've just had that I refuse to
ride home with him. I walk, a long one cause I need time
to think. The fighting continues. Even though there's no
physical violence there is always the threat of violence. I
can't stand it anymore. I need to leave. When I talk to my

best friend, my family, they all think I am overreacting. they think he's outraged because of my wild behavior. I don't talk to friends at the college cause I know how much Mack wants to protect his image. I tell him that I will tell everybody if he continues to threaten me. He boasts that he would never hit me again, that I have nothing to worry about.

Finally we just stop having talks. We see another therapist who tells us to make a recording of the kind of conversation that leads to a fight. We do. I'm shocked when we play the tape. Mack sounds so viciously violent. That does not surprise me. I am shocked by the sound of my voice. I sound like a ten-year-old girl. I never yell, shout, curse, or raise my voice. I speak in this still controlled girl voice. It frightens me. After a while the fighting stops. We both focus on school. Time passes.

Everything seems fine between them but that's just because she does not talk about her secret, that since that night she cannot stand it when he touches her. At times the feeling of panic leaves her and she enjoys being sexual with him. Mostly she feels a loss of desire. Even when she forgives him everything and she believes they are both ready to go forward she can't get her desire back. She wants to. More than anything she wants to live with Mack forever or so she says.

I remember when mama wanted to know way back when we first started to live together why aren't you marrying him. I was just nineteen but I had enough sense to say Mama, I don't know who I am really, I can't be marrying nobody. I am over thirty now. I know who I am. And I understand what's happening here. The therapist explained it too. That Mack is engaged in change—back to the way you were behavior. He wants me to be the innocent needy child-woman he fell in love with, not the powerful adult feminist woman. He reminds me more and more of mama and daddy. It just seems that all the time he's trying to break my spirit, not so I will leave him but so I will become the child-woman he fell in love with.

I'm preparing to take my Ph.D. exams again. I have told Mack how scared I am, that I need his support. We are both still committed to having an open relationship. This time I know that if things go wrong, if I am failed, I will never return to graduate school. All I do is study. I am so afraid. I have such a bad memory.

Two weeks before I take my exams Mack goes to France for a conference. I'm glad he's leaving so I can work. When he calls home I can tell something's up. He does not share anything but on the second call, when he tells me he's staying longer, I know he's met someone. I hear it in his voice, only he's not saying it. I remind him my exams are happening a few days after he comes back. I remind him that I have asked him to be there for me, to be supportive—and even though everything he says is reassuring, I can tell by the sound of his voice that something is happening. I know it must involve another woman or he would be saying what the something is.

Even though I hear something different—new—in his voice, I keep hoping that it was just a fling, that he will come home, fess up and that everything will be fine. My capacity to hope astounds.

When he walked in the door I knew when he spoke something inside me would break. He had that look— that what I have to say will crush look, maybe even break your heart, but I have to say it. And I ask him for it— straight out. He's barely closed the door and I demand to know what's really happening. He's barely crossed the threshold of the living room, into the kitchen, where I am standing by the sink, standing by a bottle of Appleton's rum. And he blurts it out: *I've met somebody. I'm in love. I'm not sure I want to continue to live with you.* The words are hardly out of his mouth before the bottle of rum's broken on the edge of the sink and I am trembling all over with the broken edge pointed at him, and all I can think about is my exams and I tell him: *Don't do this to me! If you love somebody else and want to be with them, then why did you bother to come home and tell me. Why didn't you just stay where you were. Why didn't you just stay a few more days in France with this person you love, and leave me be to study for my exams.* By now he is cleaning up the mess I have made and telling me to calm down, that we need to talk calmly.

The heated talk begins. This time there is no brutal anger. Just me trying to understand, and to make him understand why I feel he is trying to sabotage me and my exams. And that if this was really about love, his new love Tina, his old love me, that he would not be doing this. He insists that it has nothing to do with my exams, that he tried not to tell me, that I wanted to know. I can't sleep. I can't think clearly. I move through my exams in a daze.

When I do my orals, they come out to tell me not only have I passed but I've been excellent. I stand crying hysterically. The sound of my crying is so anguished I cannot bear to hear it. My primary professor puts his arms around me and says You've passed—it's all right. But I know everything is all wrong, that I could hardly write the answers on the written part because I could not stop trembling and crying.

25

My motto is "I die for style." I tell Mack that this will have to be engraved on my tombstone when I am buried. I will go to great lengths to create the environments I need. And am especially into fashion. Since I don't have any money, I buy all my clothes and everything else at secondhand stores. Fabrics and fibers intrigue me. I always wear scarves, made from huge blocks of stunning cloth. To my way of thinking it's women in Africa and India that really know the magic of a piece of cloth and the multiple things you can do with it.

Sometimes I wear cloth, take it off at the beach and use it as a blanket or a tablecloth, or sometimes you may see that same piece of cloth hanging in the window. Silk, cotton, linen, and cashmere—these are my favorites. To find the best things in secondhand stores I must always be looking. When I first went to college I bought things but it seemed like such a waste since I tired of them.

Fashion for me and my roommate then was all about seduction. We are into the art of seduction. We begin with the vamp motto that *there is no man or woman that cannot be had*. While we think it's best to stay away from folks who are already taken every now and then we fancy someone who is with someone else. The greatest challenge is to attract someone whom we desire but is apparently not interested. For this and every other act of seduction we need the right clothes. She steals them at the best stores. I am too frightened to steal but she teaches me how to change the tags.

I am into sex and clothes, so I choose clothes made of natural fibers that are earthy and sensual. Femme clothes are the least interesting to me, stuff with unnecessary ruffles and mess. I like simple elegant lines, clothes cut on the bias. Even though I hate to sew, I still do. That's why secondhand stores are the place to go. Mack thinks clothes are not important. He wears his clothes like a uniform. Now I buy for him and me.

No one at home understands my style. I like everything simple. And more and more I only wear the color black. My brother always teases that I am perpetually in mourning. That seems appropriate when I come to my poetry since all I write about is death. It's not so much the subject I chose but that subject that chooses me. No one writes great poetry about fashion. I've found this tight pink rose-colored silk blouse that just has a luscious edible quality to it. When I'm buying it I imagine someone's lips pressed against the coolness of pink silk, sucking gently leaving a stain of wetness that will not spread but stays in place. Inviting—seductive—this blouse demands recognition.

I wear it and go with Mack to hear Jerome Rothenberg read poetry. Sure enough a woman comes over to meet us afterwards. She talks to Mack about his poetry which she has already read in a journal somewhere. He's flattered by her interest. She's the type of woman he's drawn to—not conventionally beautiful but sexy and attractive in an offbeat kinda way. Later though when we have followed her home for drinks, where we meet her husband, a psychiatrist, she shares that it is the pink blouse that attracted her attention, that her husband noticed it first. Funny, this meeting since she is the type of woman Mack is drawn to and I am drawn to shrinks. This one is tall and white and drives a fast car—the kind of car I long for. That night he promises to come and take me for a drive.

Although I hate to drive, I am into cars, the beauty of design, the sound of the engine. Since living in Los Angeles I've had to learn more about the way cars work. My red Rabbit breaks down everywhere and I am constantly under the hood with strangers. It's too much. My favorite car is an old Alfa Romeo sedan. The black male lover of a white woman friend whose name I can't remember drives it. I worship at the throne of this car, even though it breaks down endlessly. Falling in love with a car that does not work properly in any sustained way is just like doing it with a lover. It breaks your heart over and over again until it just shatters and there is not

197

enough love left to see you through till the next time. I am only doing this one—going through this process with the red Rabbit and never again. Even so, when we sell it, I hurt to see it go. That's another thing about these heartbreak vehicles, it's always possible to sell them even when the true story is told. They just seduce and betray again and again.

Mack hates fancy cars. To him we just need vehicles to move us around. When I finally decide to learn how to drive a stick, it drives him nuts. After all these years of complaining about my not knowing how to drive a stick shift (even though I learned to drive on a stick shift) he's now upset that I am determined to drive this stick instead of an automatic. We have a miserable fight in front of the flirty young white salesman at the VW dealership. The guy says he will teach me to drive the stick if I buy the car. I'm ready. Mack throws the most aggressive horrible tantrum. He just refuses to support my effort to do this with no explanation other than to put me down, to suggest I've tried and I've tried before and I've never done it so why try now. This is not what I need to hear.

Suddenly as I sit crying in the parking lot alone at the dealership (Mack has decided to walk home), I see a clearly perverse and dangerous dimension to our relationship. All these years that he has made fun of me, at times contemptuously mocking me, for not driving a stick, and when I really want to learn he does not support me. I am afraid to admit that he likes me helpless in some things—dependent on him. Suddenly, I'm sitting in this parking lot remembering my first black woman friend in graduate school saying to me: *Oh! he may not mind your writing books, and even your getting your Ph.D., as long as you don't have a real job—mark my words when you get that real job he's not going be able to stand it.* I told her she did not know Mack—that he really did not care about those things, that he was into women's liberation. She just sucked her teeth and made a knowing sound. Now I have to think about all this. In this parking lot where I am facing that even though we had different skills and tasks, and different resources, I have never thought of myself as dependent on Mack (since I lived alone resourcefully before coming to live with him) and I can always see that others outside our relationship see things differently. More and more I am having to think about whether or not Mack really wants a relationship that is mutually satisfying for both partners.

When I buy the car without his support he does not speak to me for days. And it is the now obnoxious salesperson who teaches me how to drive it. Even though he's cute, he does not appeal to me. I am not a woman who likes to be seduced. I choose my men, they do not choose me. That's funny, Mack was the exception. He chose me. And I liked it at the time. I was still hurting from being rejected by Garcia, a beautiful Mexican man who worked at the day care with me, who never wanted to talk about why things between us didn't stay the same after sex. We worked together and that made not talking hard. I got involved with Mack right after that. It felt good to be chosen.

Mack will not speak to me for days after I buy the car.

He says I humiliated him in the eyes of this salesman. I say: *Who gives a fuck about him and what he thinks. He's not in this relationship.* But that's another thing I have to face about me and Mack. He cares so much about how other people see things. I don't care what other people see—especially people I don't know.

Now when we go places, Mack cannot make a big deal out of the fact that he must do the driving. Since he hated to drive the automatic and usually refused to do so we would always take his car. Now we can take either one of the cars. He still likes driving his car best. I could care less. I like to stay home.

26

Leaving Los Angeles all I can think about is that I will be thirty in a few years and the first book that I finished writing at nineteen, rewriting it for years, before I put it high up on a closet shelf, is coming down. It's in my hands again. I think it's time for me to go back to it, rewrite some more and start again. I have also decided I can go back to graduate school, to finish my Ph.D.

Although Mack will respect any decision I make, he tells me again and again that to try to get employed in the university system with just a master's degree (which I have now) will get me nowhere. He reminds me that it's important to have a Ph.D., especially if you are more interested in creative writing. Since basically the hard-core academics have no respect for creative writing. And even though I imagine I will live with him forever, I certainly face every day the reality that without a Ph.D. I teach the same number of classes and don't make nearly the same amount of money. Luckily for me Santa Cruz accepts some of my credits so it will not take me as long as it did the last time to get to the exams.

She applies to this fancy new program they have started at Santa Cruz that is interdisciplinary. It has just the right focus. But when she goes to interview with a professor he lets her know that she is not "theoretical" enough. She knew she was not going to be accepted when he tried to force her to identify herself as Marxist, socialist-feminist, poststructuralist, or any label and she kept saying she considered them tools to use, even perspectives that might help illuminate one's work. Her not claiming a fixed standpoint evidently indicated a lack of seriousness. She is also told that the one black woman they had admitted in the past was having difficulty finishing her dissertation, and had begun to feel that the program was not right for her.

Anytime one black student has difficulty or fails, every black student that comes after will be seen as flawed and looked at with suspicion. No matter how many white students fail for whatever reason they will still be looked at as individuals. This is racism in America. It never stops. I came to Santa Cruz with Mack to look it over to see if it was a place for me. I fall in love with this small city—the sea, the greenery, the bougainvillea everywhere. It just has a magical feel about it. The campus does not interest

202

me. It's just too much like summer camp. And of course lest we forget the history of racism and imperialism, those of us who are different are constantly reminded by everyone talking about this campus as the city on the hill. I have to go into the literature program, the same program Mack works for. That's a drag. We both would like things to be a little more separate so what I do does not impact on him and vice versa. In the past I've usually been the target when any more powerful academic does not like him. I hate institutions and how they function. The only reason I'm going back to graduate school is that there is no work here. I've had all these ridiculous part-time jobs.

And even though the last job was fun (cooking at the jazz club) where I get to listen to all the great musicians and meet them too. I get to meet Sun Ra, Archie Shepp. Although the "girls" in the kitchen don't get talked to that much, especially if you are black, when I cook the musicians do come back for more and more food, especially desserts. My lemon tarts are a total favorite. Mama does not believe I can really cook since I never went near the kitchen growing up. She says I never wanted to help but what I remember is being told all the time that I was too stupid when it came to practical things to know how to do anything. Mama would say I was in her way.

I didn't start cooking until I began to live with Mack. He shows me how. At first we just made all the wonderful dishes his ex-girlfriend used to make for him and she was, he says, a fantastic cook. She leaves him with a spiral notebook full of his favorite recipes all of which he learns to cook. Although he never cooked when they lived together. Now we take turns. I cook one week and he cooks the next. I can't cook anything without a recipe. But show me any recipe in a cookbook and I can cook it. I like to cook food from all over the world but my favorite country is India. Sometimes we eat Indian cooking every day of the week. Vegetarian Indian is the best— cauliflower curry, okra, eggplant with assorted home-made chutneys and pickles.

Working all the time leaves me no time to write. That's when I started to think about going back to school. When we first moved to Santa Cruz I didn't think school was for me. But more and more I see Mack is right—with just a master's degree I'll always be working too hard for too little and I add to this never have time to really write. I take the small service porch in the house we have rented from a horrible divorced white English professor who lives behind us in a new place he built on the property and make it into a tiny office for me. It's there I sit to go over my manuscript *Ain't I a Woman: Black Women and Feminism* for what I have decided will be the last time. Reading over it after the years it spent resting in the closet, I see some of the problems. I am trying to accommodate too many perspectives in that way we learn in graduate school. And not choosing to write the polemical piece I want to write. I begin another edit—the final one. This time though I believe someone will publish this book.

Taking feminist theory in graduate school, I am no

longer the shy silent student I was at Stanford, afraid to bring up the issue of race. This time I talk and disagree and will not back down. Now that I am years older, I don't believe anymore that white females in this country do not understand that their status and as a consequence their lives are very different from those of black females. Often when I try to bring up the way race changes the theories that are being set forth solely and absolutely in the name of common gender—we are all female and thus share a similiar fate—it's me against a whole class of white women. Yet in the classes I teach when I ask students to imagine they die and can be born again choosing their race and gender and they write their choices, no one not even black females wants to come back black and female. When asked why everyone can talk about why it's harder. More people want to come back as white men. It's always funny for me to imagine what this world would look like or even feel like if it was peopled mainly by white men. It's a scary thought. On many levels white men remain a mystery to me.

I am surviving this time in graduate school without having major conflicts with professors, everyone is nicer here than anywhere else we have been. It's still hard. Classes are so boring. And all that unnecessary writing of long papers. I will say one positive thing about that professor I longed to kill, he was always telling us that it was a total mistake to write long twenty- and thirty-page papers because no journal would ever publish them and we should really write succinct clear ten-page papers or shorter—that this was a real writing challenge. He was right. I hate writing about subjects that don't interest me and wish there was some other way we could be evaluated.

In my feminist literature class we are reading Pauline Réage, *The Story of O*. I want to write a paper on the way in which the book creates a symbolic narrative of colonialism. When I give my presentation in class, everyone is again annoyed that I don't want to seem to deal "just" with gender. I keep saying there is no world where just gender matters. It's funny, the only world I have been in where I could focus almost exclusively on patterns of gendered domination was when I was living at home within a structure of racial apartheid. Since white folks were never present in our domestic lives it was possible to see all issues of power solely in relationship to sex roles. That's why I think it was there that I began to create patriarchy and not out in the world somewhere. The moment anybody black moves out into the world somewhere, away from segregation, we always have to think about the ways race matters, sometimes more than gender, sometimes the same as gender, but always in convergence and collusion. It's the connectedness of race and gender that the white students and teachers in the classroom want to deny. That's why it becomes so clear to me that they think of feminism as this little colony that they own—that is their property, just like lots of black men felt like the Civil Rights movement, and Black Power struggle, belonged more to them than to women.

If I did not have Mack to go home to and discuss

everything with it would be a miserable life. I am sure I would just quit. He understands the interconnections of race and gender. Only he doesn't understand why I need to share my ideas in the classroom, why I need to be heard. He thinks I would spare myself a lot of pain if I would just sit in these classrooms and be silent.

27

Writing is my passion. Words are the way to know ecstasy. Without them life is barren. The poet insists *Language is a body of suffering and when you take up language you take up the suffering too.* All my life I have been suffering for words. Words have been the source of the pain and the way to heal.

Struck as a child for talking, for speaking out of turn, for being out of my place. Struck as a grown woman for not knowing when to shut up, for not being willing to sacrifice words for desire. Struck by writing a book that disrupts. There are many ways to be hit. Pain is the price we pay to speak the truth. *Language is a body of suffering and when you take up language you take up the suffering too.*

Nothing is as simple as it seems, so much is neither good nor bad, but always a blend of truths. In the household of my childhood, that place where I was held prisoner, there was no doubt in anyone's mind that I would write, that I would become a writer, magician of words, one who suffers well. *She works hard in the name of love. She who is able to sacrifice.*

Nothing is as simple as it seems. No one in the house of my childhood doubts my power to create. I learn doubt when I leave home. I learn to doubt my intelligence, my creativity in the integrated world—at college and in the arms of talented men. They try and teach me to fear a woman's word, to doubt whether her words can ever be as good, as perfect as any man's sound. No wonder then there is something in me that clings to childhood—to the girl who loved Emily Dickinson, writer, thinker, dreamer of worlds. In the shadow of her presence, I am without doubt. I know I can become a writer.

She stayed with him much longer than she should have. Her staying was never a way to cling to love. She feared losing the discipline to write. She entered a committed relationship so soon, so young devote herself to writing. So much in the world distracted her from words. So much made life seem crazy. At times she dreamed of returning home. Despite all the madness of home, she had always found a place to read, contemplate life, and write there.

She is right. Nothing is as simple as it seems. You would think all those fancy colleges she went to so far away from home would have made it easy to write. Baba used to asked her How can you live so far away from your people. At home she doubted her capacity to love, to be intimate, to make friends even. Introverted and awkward she doubted so much about herself but never her ability to imagine, to write.

No one really says how it will be. When we try to leave behind all the limits of race and gender and class, to transcend them, to get to the heart of the matter. No one really says how painful it will be—that just when you think you are moving forward in life some new thing, another barrier surfaces that just stops you in your tracks. For all that goes wrong in my life with Mack, I have had shelter here, a sanctuary for that part of me that was destined to write, to make a life in words. *Language is a body of suffering and when you take up language you take up the suffering too.*

Nobody ever talked to us about how we would become these new women and men transformed by feminist movement. All the cultural revolutions created by black liberation and sexual liberation and women's liberation, and yet there is still no map—nothing that will guide us safely to mutual love and respect. We lose our way. One thing is certain—we can never turn back.

After all our feminist victory, there is still a grave silence about the issue of whether women can be in love relationships with men and truly develop as writers. I believe my relationship with Mack strengthens me as a thinker and a writer. I used to say that we were better at giving each other the space to be independent than we were at being together. I grew stronger as a writer at all times, even during times when we were in crisis. Writing was my refuge and my rescue.

She believed for so long that if she left their relationship she might cease to write. After all she became a disciplined published writer there in the shadows of their love. To depart from that love might mean to depart from writing. She could imagine living without him. She could not imagine living without words. And so she remained.

They all wanted to know *Why did you stay with him so long.* I am weary explaining. Doesn't everyone realize that nothing is as simple as it seems. Our relationship falling apart is no one's fault. Everybody wants somebody to blame. I wanted to make sense of the pain. The ways I was hurt in this relationship and the ways I hurt were only one fragment of a larger piece. When I left home, I thought I was leaving hurt behind. I did not even imagine that there were ways to be hurt in the world outside home. When you are confined to a small segregated area across the tracks, away from so much going on in the larger world, innocence is still possible. Measured against the pain in the world, home seemed a safe haven, both the home I left and the home I had made with Mack.

To explain things she says: Every terrorist regime in the world uses isolation to break the human spirit. It is not difficult for her to see that women writers, especially black women writers, are isolated. She can count the ones whose work is recognized. She can see for herself how many die alone, unloved, their work forgotten. She can see for herself how many remain invisible. She can see how many go mad.

Haunted by the fear of madness, I am deeply convinced that the world is not a safe place for me. I remain reluctant to move, to change, to go anywhere. I need company to move outside the home. That was the way it was growing up. A girl was never left alone. When I came to college I realized I had never been alone not even for a day. Whenever we left the house as girls we were escorted. In private I love to be alone. In public I prefer company.

They were always so together the two of them. They did everything together. No wonder then it was surprising that they could not work together in the same room. In private they were alone, they were silent. In private they were devoted to work.

Women sacrifice for words. They suffer and they die. The poet Audre Lorde visits our house. She sits and flirts on our Victorian deep red couch. She has just autographed a copy of my favorite poem "Litany for Survival." Her words say everything there is to say about the perils the exploited and the oppressed face coming to voice.

She goes straight to the heart of the matter: *When we are loved we are afraid love will vanish / when we are alone we are afraid love will never return / and when we speak we are afraid our words will not be heard not welcome / but when we are silent we are still afraid.*

28

We fight about money. No matter how hard I work I
make less money. He spends money on his passions—
books and records. I spend money on the household
mainly, sometimes on clothes. Often at the end of the
month we are in debt—total debt. We end up borrowing
money. He borrows from his mother. He borrows from
his uncle who has a thousand business deals going legal
and illegal. I am not into borrowing. For me it's a matter
of pride. We are grown—time to take care of ourselves,
not to burden our folks, who should be able to keep all
their money for themselves.

*He tells her she does not understand that America is all
about debt. That to borrow and owe is the American way.
She doesn't care about any of this. She believes in paying
her way—with cash. If they want to buy something she*

thinks they should save until they can do it, not go into debt, not borrow from others. She likes to save, having grown up in a house where a mother was always putting a little bit away for a rainy day. Only Rosa Bell never told the truth about money, knowing that if you tell folks what you have they will spend it for you. Or if you let a husband know that you have a little money put away he will make sure he withholds just that amount. And soon your little bit of money will be all gone.

I had money problems once, buying clothes. As a college student I got sent credit cards. That's how I ran up that clothing debt. I told myself I needed clothes for work—straight-looking clothes—suits. I bought them and hardly ever wore them. I don't like form-fitting clothes—straight-looking clothes. They sat in my closet for a long minute before I gave them away. And there I was—left with all that debt.

Money was a constant problem in their household growing up. Mr. Veodis was as secretive about what he did with his money as most men—and then some. Like every black man he was working at a job where the white folks weren't really paying him his due. That would eventually change with all them antidiscrimination laws but all that took a while and she already away. Now his income was good but his family was large and he gave Rosa Bell only so much money. At times her mama had to beg and scrape. Her daddy just couldn't understand the needs of children today. He was always bringing up when he got by on little and was happy.

Her daddy Mr. Veodis had been one of them playboy-type men who married late, and he was not used to sharing his money or to withholding his own pleasure. So he always had his little toys. Lord, that man loved gadgets, cameras, movie projectors, and the like—anything electronic. He was not into sharing these pleasures with his family. It was rare for him to open up and share. He liked to keep things to himself. Well, he was his mother's only child.

I hated all the discussion about money growing up. The way we were all made to feel guilty about needing anything, even schoolbooks were a problem. Somehow we were made to feel that it was our fault that things cost so much. Every single one of us learned early on that if we wanted something there was no point in asking daddy cause he was not gonna understand. He was not going to even think about satisfying your desire. Now mama, approaching her was a different story altogether. We used to think it was because she was so close to being young that she just seemed to understanding longings. If she could she would help fulfill them. She worked magic to make us happy. She worked around daddy's selfishness. I knew too watching her I was never going to depend on any man to give me money.

She was into things because she was clear that things cost and she knew that she did not want to pay the price. Even

216

as a little bitty child she kept her longings simple. And even then they were rarely satisfied. Instead of getting what she wanted for Christmas or birthdays she was always getting what they thought she should have. She used to wonder why did they even bother to ask. The crazy thing was she kept believing that she would really get the things she wanted. Maybe that was cause everyone and then her mama would get that one special something she desired. But mostly she watched as the others had their desires filled. She was left out of the mix.

I love to give presents—to give something that is truly desired. I have a Native American woman friend who lives in Silver Lake and she teaches me that it is good to give something you love away especially if it is admired or longed for by someone else. She gives me a beautiful black crystal vase—as collecting glass is her special pleasure. With her I am completely at home. Even though we think differently about the roles of women and men (she has no use for feminism), for her the issue is land rights, Indian rights, fighting genocide. Even though she does not claim the term feminism or the movement, it is clear that she struggles equally with the men of her community for freedom. We talk and read together. We talk about the ways the black struggles for self-determination and Native American struggle overlap. We teach each other and love each other.

Mack thinks she is way too self-righteous and her man even more so. He thinks it's crazy to give away things you love. When we first meet I am never bothered by his lack of generosity. I understand the way growing up in a home where there are issues around money can corrupt. I believe he will change in time. He tells stories of slipping records and books into the house so his mother does not see them. A woman alone raising children, working hard, she sees no place for small pleasures. To her they are unnecessary luxuries. She reminds me of my daddy. They share the same birthday and were born in the same year. It's a generational thing. Mack remembers being yelled at and punished for small pleasures and he carries those memories with pain.

She is so blind. She can't see how much like Mr. Veodis Mack is. He never wants to share. And in some ways he is worse than Mr. Veodis. No matter how many times she shares that presents matter, he will not give gifts, or he will give something she could not possibly ever want. When she gives him special things like that out of print My Name Is Albert Ayler *record he has always wanted (that she has to search and search to find) he never shows he is pleased. He punishes her for the past, like he cannot see her as someone other than his mother. Holidays with him are as miserable for her as they were at home. Though she does everything to create the perfect home— the perfect atmosphere of warmth and love—he shatters it with his discontent. To him communal pleasure means nothing. He likes to keep his pleasure to himself just like Mr. Veodis. She sees none of this. She thinks it is her— that there is something she is doing wrong. It takes her a long time to look critically at him.*

218

I take a stand. We have to depend on ourselves and our
own resources. I refuse to borrow from others and
demand that he do the same. We keep a budget. We take
our income and decide that I will pay a third and he will
pay two thirds, that we will have separate accounts and
joint household accounts. I work lots of little jobs, work
long hours and am often tired. It's hard to come up with
my one third but I do not want to depend on him. I think
I should work. He tells me often that it's fine if I want to
take time off—that he can pay the bills and take care of
everything. I am afraid of all forms of economic depen-
dency. I would rather work. Finally we stop fighting
about money.

29

Nowadays the *Ain't I a Woman* manuscript is off the shelf and all over my desk. I am doing the final rewrite. If I don't find a publisher this time I am giving up. The cultural mood is different now. That makes me hopeful. When I was first trying to find a publisher to take the book seriously I kept being told by "insiders" that there was just no audience to talk about race and feminism or black women and feminism. Everything is changing now. Even though I still encounter some hostility in my graduate classes trying to talk about race, the topic is out there. It's being discussed.

It comes as no surprise to me that the feminist white women I know who are most willing to take on the issue of race are lesbians. Some do it because they came out of working in civil rights struggle and others because they know what it feels like to have your identity not be taken seriously. There is this cute white woman who works at the museum in Berkeley. We keep seeing each other at different events. She works in the restaurant where they have the best carrot cake in the world. Even though we keep seeing each other at feminist stuff, we really start talking in the restaurant. On the night that I plan to talk about my work at the women's bookstore in San Francisco, she comes. Then later she comes down to Santa Cruz with a group of women to hang out—everybody's white but what else is new.

Mack is the only man present at the women's bookstore when I talk about my work. The room is packed. Because he's a black man he is even more visible. Nobody cares about his being there though. I can see he feels self-conscious. And I was even okay with him not coming if he didn't want to be in the total woman space thing. There are a few black women, a couple of my students, present. Betty, the one I like best, is here. She looks like a model, tall, thin, absolutely gorgeous. That "girl" can wear some lipstick. She always has on military clothing cause she's in the reserves. Older than most of us, she's back in school after serving overseas in the army. I begin by talking about the ways acknowledging race changes how we can talk about gender, just stating the basic idea that "work" liberates—so that we can talk about the limitation of this idea for women who work really low-paying jobs and have families to support. It's a class thing too. Much of my perspective has been shaped by coming from a working-class background where there was never enough money. I talk about the overlap of race and class. When I'm done reading the section from the book I've chosen to highlight, the one about the continued devaluation of black women, the discussion is just crazy with tension and conflict, so much resistance to the idea of race. When I'm attacked Betty backs me up. She's totally out as a lesbian so nobody can do that dismiss the straight woman cause she doesn't really get it thing.

At one point I feel so frustrated I could cry. It's like everything I've been experiencing in the classroom and more. White women can't even face their hostility at having to listen to a black woman talk when she's saying what they don't want to hear. They think it's just the ideas. Most of them have never listened to a black woman, or taken anything a black woman says seriously. Even the white girls who were in the civil rights movement were always idolizing the black women they worked with, competing with them, turning then into mammy (as in Take care of me and show me what to do), seeing how they suffer and still idolizing. Nobody likes it when I say: Idolatry can be just another way to dehumanize black women.

On the long drive home, Mack tells me my talk was incredible, that he fell in love with me all over again just listening to me deal with the crowd. He goes on and on about how he can't get over the way I changed from being the really quiet and intense person I am at home, to this person who speaks with such authority. The talk exhausts me. I feel sick inside. Mack knows I am not entirely comfortable with public speaking, particularly speaking about political stuff. He knows that I am uncertain about whether it's a good thing I am spending less time thinking about poetry—the writer's life—and more time thinking about feminism and the role of women. It's a hard choice. It's hard to do everything. The more I get into feminism, the more poetry becomes a private thing I steal time to do. Still, I feel that the spirits of all my ancestors, the women in my family, want me to do this, to speak out. I accept this because I see it as a divine calling even though it does not express the innermost me. Mack and I talk endlessly about the struggle I am having, trying to forge my own identity.

Luckily, my women friends struggle with the same issues. We all flock around this really beautiful Italian sociologist Laura who is a visiting professor. Those of us who remain romantically involved with men, even if we see ourselves as bisexual, find it refreshing to have a political woman (a member of parliament), who's also married and has children, sharing with us her work and life. She's so open. We can ask her anything. My closest friend in our circle is Marijke, a Dutch woman who lives in my neighborhood. We tease each other that we are friends because we both love desserts. She is always telling me how good the cakes are in Holland, that I have to come visit and see for myself. We eat on these hand-painted plates she got as a wedding present. I like them cause they have chickens hand-painted on them, and they make me think of home, of the country. Our lesbian friends tease me that I'm from the country and can't tell the difference between a rooster and a hen. That's the real image on the wedding plates. We are also both into flowers. Every time she comes to visit she brings flowers. Naturally my favorites are tulips, and naturally the best, the most wonderful tulips can be found in Holland.

When Mack and I finally bought a little house with a red door, the huge backyard was full of weeds. I was determined to plant trees and grow grass. After the first time we spent weeks digging (with Mack doing most of the dirty work) and our grass did not grow, he refused to have anything more to do with this project. The next time I called all my feminist friends and invited them to a weed pulling, digging, planting grass party. Only Marijke showed up dressed to kill. She refused to change. When the sun got hot she took off the fancy cotton blouse she was wearing and worked in the sexiest black bra we had ever seen. This was too much for me. I had grown up in the hard-core world of Sunday clothes versus everyday clothes. I couldn't believe she felt we should look good no matter what we were doing, and wear what we like— since it could be washed. I was so impressed. From that day forth I was determined to make no distinctions and just wear whatever I wanted to when I wanted to wear it. After working we sat around eating, drinking, and talking about the usual feminist issues.

The next week I was back at the Berkeley museum talking to my new girlfriend there who told me about this ad she'd found in the local feminist newspaper. It was placed by alternative press collective South End Press and they were advertising for manuscripts about race and feminism. That weekend she and a bunch of women, mostly lesbians, came and hung out on the beach. We talked endlessly about lesbianism and feminism, about the fundamental fact that the deeper you go into challenging sexism the harder it is to be with men. She gives me the ad she told me about and makes me promise I will write them right away. I do. Ellen, "speaking for the press," promptly writes back and tells me they want to see the manuscript and later that they want to publish it. I can't believe it! Finally after all the hard work somebody is interested. Of course, there's no money involved but who cares. That's why I have jobs so I don't have to make money with writing, so I can write what I want to write.

Even though I am pleased that they want to publish the book, in our first conversation Ellen and I disagree. She tells me that she and the rest of the collective think that the book is too angry. I share that I think the book is blunt, clear, but that does not mean anger, that this is one of the issues around race, and racial difference, that every time I speak directly, white girls think I am angry. In the same way that they don't like the word girl. They don't understand it as a term of endearment, when women use it with one another. Girl as in girlfriend. As in when mama says to me "little girl" or when I say to one of my sisters "girl." I tell Ellen, my editor to be—young, white, lesbian—that we can work on making changes, I'm willing to do that, but I know when I am speaking from anger and when I am not. Like, me, she and the press are into processing. It's a good beginning. When she comes to California we meet. Ellen has a good heart, a loving heart. Even when we vehemently disagree, we find a way to make it through the process.

I need to work with and for folks I respect. I want to know the South End Press collective—to enter their world and be a part of it. It's John who does the accounting I talk to the most. When we start talking on the phone because I'm complaining about money, I think he's a woman. Not only because he has one of those sometimes gender neutral voices but because he is always talking about taking care of his daughter. I talk openly with him about my concerns, about my health, this female body that fails me so much. When I realize he's a man we both freak. He reminds that he always spoke of his wife. And I replied lots of lesbians I know talk about their wives. This was the first time in my life that I fully realized that I share differently when I'm talking to a man. If anyone had ever tried to tell me that I would have said No I relate to people in the same way. As I slowly get to know people at the press I like some better than others but it's a publishing home for me. I feel respected and safe there. I like everything the collective stands for and just want them to include more people of color. We still fight about things (like the cover) which I think I've put together and a design credit is given to Ellen. Why Ellen and not me. Little things we fight about, and big things.

When Ellen wants me to write about lesbianism differently than the way I do, I refuse. It's not the subject. I refuse to add anything new. I've worked myself to the bone on this book and frankly there is not any juice left. I agree with Ellen that to say critical things about lesbians within feminist movement without saying positive things could perpetuate homophobia so we remove the critical comments. Later when the book is reviewed I will be accused of being so homophobic that I can not bring myself to say the word lesbian. Since I have always been there to fight for sexual freedom this wounds me more than any other critique. I can't believe I will be judged and condemned on the basis of things that are absent. It's one thing to critique that absence; it's another thing for folks who don't know to insist that their explanation for an absence is the truth. This willingness to accuse and condemn without all the facts discourages me; it's a dangerous thread I see running through feminist movement.

South End calls to tell me that they are sending a hot off the press first copy of the book to me. When it comes, my first feeling as I stand on the threshold of a wide open red door, book in hand, is that it's strange not to see my real name on the cover. I think all my friends and everyone I went to school with will never know it's me. Suddenly, it hits me. Using the pseudonym bell hooks has really worked. My ego cannot be as identified with this book. It's strangely satisfying and disappointing.

Mack is working in his study. When I rush in with the book, he does not stop work. He holds his head up for a second to register its presence. I suggest we go out later to celebrate and he answers maybe. For a moment he takes the wind out of my sails. I leave his study and go upstairs and call my friends. All the pleasure returns. My first book—in my hands.

She is so used to building walls that can keep the hurt away, she can't see his desire to negate her moment of pleasure. She really believes it's because he is busy. She's never been able to see the basic competitiveness that is his character. This is her narcissism. Being such a loner in childhood, she is not used to competing with others. Hers is always an inner challenge, to live up to the standards she sets for herself. She loves it when he succeeds so she can only imagine he wants the same for her. She can't even see that he supported her writing so much because he never believed anyone other than him would take it seriously.

It's a strange evening. We quarrel about whether or not to go out. Mack is coldly withdrawn and indifferent. It's like I'm a divided soul—part of me is working overtime to make it a celebratory moment and another part of me is crushed that sadness is here, taking over even at my moment of triumph. This is nothing new. It always happened this way in childhood. Just at all those times when I should have been celebrating and having fun, something would always go wrong and I would end up hurt inside. That's why I dread holidays and most other celebratory times. I like birthdays and the new year. Mack never really says anything about the book.

Later though he lets me know that he is pissed that in the acknowledgments I thank him for being helpful some of the time, or something like that. To my mind I told the truth. Sometimes he hated my writing the book and complained and stood in the way and put me down. And then other times he helped but mostly he helped in the beginning. I think it is important to be truthful—to tell the truth and nothing but the truth.

Even though I wrote the first draft at nineteen it's taken almost ten years for this book to come into being. I am so excited. Now I can move on. First I have to deal with graduate school. I am writing my dissertation on Toni Morrison. My colleague at San Francisco State where I commute to teach, Angela Davis, knows her and says we should meet each other. I agree. But I don't ever plan on meeting Toni Morrison before I get this dissertation written. Too many things go wrong when I meet people. I know if I looked into her heart and did not like what I saw there I wouldn't be able to go on writing about her first two books which fascinate me—*The Bluest Eye* and *Sula*. The best thing about writing on Toni Morrison is that there is not a lot of primary material available about her work so I have to think for myself. That is such a challenge. It's great. I read these two books over and over, hundreds of times, each time there is something new to be discovered in the writing. I learn so much from Toni Morrison's work.

Writing the dissertation, I realize being a literary critic is not my destiny. I want to write books that everybody can read. I want to write books that move outside the world of the academy. It surprises me when I am attacked for not using footnotes in *Ain't I a Woman*. When I was writing the book I just went around talking to the women I thought the book was for, like my friends who are still working at the phone company, and they all said they never read books with footnotes—that they think these books are not for them. After talking with women outside academia I abandon the hundreds of note cards with footnotes. South End does not agree with this decision, but I did it with the hope of crossing boundaries. Now everyone is acting like this is an act of treason. Yet in my literary criticism classes we read those books by French critics that have no footnotes and no one ever finds that weird. It's an absence that is never even mentioned. We are too busy drooling over the great writing and the great ideas. I'm drooling too. I love reading Barthes and the rest. It's another boundary to cross. Funny no one seems to want to cross boundaries that take them away from Europe. When they do everything is suspect.

It's weird to be a graduate student when you have written and published a book. I am respected and at the same a suspect. In academia you are always "suspect" any time you are not in step with the usual procedures, any time you don't conform. That's why I know it's not the world for me. I want to write more books. Mack convinced me I need the Ph.D. to get a job. That having a job will give me the space to write, summers at least. I know he's right. He reminds me again and again that so many writers who try to making a living from selling work end up writing what other people want them to write just to make a buck. Having a job will let me write what I want to write. That's real artistic freedom.

30

We have quickly become deeply involved in Robert Duncan's life. Everything I dream about in relationship to the aesthetics of an artist's life is personified by the marriage between him and Jess, his lover. They like to say they've been together so many years they's stopped counting. We were surprised and pleased when we first went to Robert's house because he lived in the Mission. Most white people we know don't like the Mission. We make the long drive up from Santa Cruz to eat in Cuban restaurants with Robert, to have the best Mexican food, to drink beer and talk about poetry and myth.

As always I am a listener. Robert is ecstatic about our right to live a life centered on poetry and poetics. He can write with glee: *Working in words I am an escapist; as if I could step out of my clothes and move naked as the wind in a world of words.* In our house we make jokes about not wanting to be around when Robert decides to really step out of his clothes. He came to dinner and as he talked about myth and poetry, he stripped his shirt off. He was feeling the heat, the passion of his whirlwind of words. When Duncan talks I am reminded of Sufi dancing as he whirls and whirls and whirls you with words so that you are finally there in that ecstatic place where you have left the body behind and entered that magic place where there is no flesh—no identity.

We meet Robert at a time in his life when real-life identities are encroaching on his mythic past. Adopted long ago, he finds out there are siblings in the world wanting to know him. He is nervous to make this real-life contact with those with whom he shares blood but possibly nothing else. A long-lost sister finds him through something in the press. Already the relatives know more about him than he knows about them. In his old age this is a new and exciting adventure. We hang on for the ride as Duncan goes in search of parts of himself he did not know existed.

He is the center of all our dialogue. Mack and I are not at all disturbed by this. We have both been raised in a culture where elders claim center stage. Used to listening, to serving, we are more than willing to worship at his throne. Sometimes, but rarely, he wants to know what is happening with Mack. He wants to know nothing about me. Mack interests him because he is a handsome sexy young man. We are charmed that, no matter his age, Robert still loves to be publicly seen walking arm and arm with a lovely man.

I come along on these trips not so much to spend time

with Robert Duncan but to worship at the feet of his lover Jess, who is as close to a saint in my imagination as a human can come. When I look into his heart the first time we meet I see such tenderness there I want to weep, to hold him in my arms. His inner tenderness is a closely guarded paradise. Before we meet him we have heard about Jess. Not so much from Robert though but from the poets we hang out with who know them, and from what Mack has read. What we have heard is what intrigues me. That Jess rarely leaves the house except to search in various and sundry places for stuff to make art with; that unlike Robert he rarely speaks.

We know we have finally been accepted by Robert when our visits to the huge Victorian house in the Mission are no longer restricted to ringing the bell and waiting on the steps for Duncan to come down. Jess is the mystery voice we hear on the other side. When we see him he looks like your average middle-class white businessman or academic, only his heart is nowhere near the world of academia or business. It's hard even to imagine him the chemist he used to be.

Here in the Mission, Jess and Robert have created a dwelling place for spirits, an awesome home, where together they have shaped an aesthetics of existence, an art of life. The first floor is communal space, full of antiques and art. Pasteups by Jess, who says he's more comfortable with that term than the more fashionable word collage. There are a whole series of witty black and white pasteups that are no-smoking signs. They are the first hint that Jess has a wicked sense of humor behind the saintly smile and demeanor.

Despite the richness of the decor, there is always an aura of contemplation in this house. It's a space where excess is balanced by temperance and pleasure by self-discipline. This is the first and major lesson I will learn from being in the presence of the artist Jess (the art of discipline) who will become—unbeknownst to him—one of my great teachers in life. The Vietnamese Buddhist Thich Nhat Hanh has already taught me in his work that really great teachers do not have to say anything—that merely to be in their presence is to be in a space where it is possible to learn.

I learn by looking. Jess shows me the world where he works. And tells me how he rises early every day to be in that space, committed to a certain quality of light that he will have only so many hours in the day. To nurture his relationship to that light, and the work it allows him to make, he must be devoted. Second lesson—devotion. So far discipline and devotion. Even before I know him better I am beginning to rethink whether or not I am truly ready to be a real artist. Can I be disciplined and devoted.

Then there is the issue of attention. The third lesson to bring all one's energies and awareness to bear on the moment by being undivided in one's attention, to be fully present to the art you are making. Fully present when he is making art—undivided—and fully present when he is making lunch or dinner which I will watch him do often over the years. I never cook for Jess since he is not a traveling man, not a man for scenes or crowds. When you see him, though, he is fully present. I want to learn this, the art of being present—how to be here now.

31

Finally, even though I have always dreamed of turning away from the world, of living a fundamentally contemplative life, I have never thought about the ways one is changed by turning away. To turn inward, as Jess does, is in some ways to lose touch. Losing touch matters for Jess because in that space of loss he imaginatively constructs the new world, an alternative universe.

She has been troubled for so long about what it means to want to be devoted to the artistic life and at the same time have intense committed relationships. Seeing Jess and Robert together gives her hope. They represent for her the ideal—mutual partnership, closeness yet autonomy, differentiation of status without subordination. That their love can open up to include friendships, lovers, an array of people not like themselves. Their gayness is both significant and not solely defining. This is how she wants to feel about blackness, that it can always be significant without being the only aspect of her identity that matters. The same is true of being a woman. Despite the obstacles women face trying to be devoted to art practice, she believes it is possible to move past domination and triumph. This moving past will not be easy. Any more than it has been easy for Robert to be gay and out before the culture was ready and welcoming. And yet he dared it. She feels so lucky to be a witness to this life.

Sometimes when the four of us are together, I feel we are blessed to not have let race, or gender, or age, or differences in temperament keep us from connecting. Sometimes when we come to the city and stay on the very top floor of Robert and Jess's world, lying on old-fashioned crisp cold white cotton sheets, it does feel like a dream. That the world outside has not really changed, has not broken down barriers but here in the interior life, in that aesthetics of existence where the power to create lies in our hands, all is possible. Art creates a space where we can transcend.

Jess is the one person in my life who encourages me not to give up painting. Even though he has not seen my work, he assures me that I can write and make art. He knows that I painted as a child, that I loved abstract expressionists with a passion. Robert and I talk about art, works we like and don't like.

My favorite work of Jess's is not the huge pasteup that hangs in the studio, which he has labored on for years, cutting, arranging, and creating images. I like the small pieces. My favorite—titled simply "alone in a crowd." To have the money to buy work, to own art, is one of my dreams. Coming to see Jess and Robert has taught me the importance of supporting artists by buying their work even if one pays just a little month by month. They are always supporting someone, exchanging art, collaborating, and buying outright. Their collection is full of stories, each piece lets us know something about the direction of their life.

Complete utter devotion to art-making never alienates Jess from the simple tasks of life. In this way he seems to me such a Buddhist (though he never has anything good to say about organized religion or any institution for that matter). He's just a free spirit, unattached and yet bound. Like me, he hates crowds. Unlike me he can go to the museums and look at shows when no one is around, when the doors are closed to the public. Now that's a luxury.

Sometimes Robert makes art. This inspires me. Already I know writing is my primary passion but making art can still be there as a space to enter beyond words. The Berkeley museum does a show about his work "the poet as artist" that is deeply moving. There are self-portraits he has drawn, images he has painted. There is no way he can live with art and not want to move beyond words, into a space where only one the eye speaks. Jess never says anything to us about Robert's art.

It excites me that they are so different. Robert is such an exhibitionist, always taking center stage. Jess is content to be in the shadows. He does not stand there because he is passive or subordinate but because that is the place where he is most comfortable. Photographs of them show this difference, Robert directly out front and Jess somewhere close by but always just a little behind. Some people think Robert dominates Jess. Yet when you get to know them it is clear that Jess is always choosing. That's the point, not that everything in a marriage or partnership be equal but that each person has the right, the power, and the freedom to choose.

Robert needs flirtations, seductions, and the possibilities of endless love. He goes out in the world roaming and Jess stays home. Somehow though because they are both men, and white men, this difference seems less threatening than when one is a woman with a man preferring solitary home life. In patriarchal culture it's too easy for this to become a situation of domination and submission, a situation where the man moves freely and the woman has no choice. Apparently, Jess has no interest in all that Robert does when he is away from home. Nothing we see suggests Jess has not claimed fully the space of his serenity.

For him painting is the spiritual process. Again and again he testifies that he does not see that much difference between the spiritual and the material: *All matter is energy, and all matter and energy are infused with spirit.* There is a sweet sweet spirit in this house where Robert and Jess live, this space that they have created for love and work. I want to have such a house. Yet Mack seems

240

much less interested in making a world where one lives an aesthetics of existence. The visual does not interest him that much. In that way I am more like Robert than he is.

Duncan and I are interested in everything—all the arts. We want to know about everything. He and Jess love opera. During my first semester at Stanford I go to the opera for the first time in my life. A group of students buy cheap tickets. Our seats are lousy but we can hear just fine. Mack loves all kinds of music, and so do I but Robert and Jess have more conventional music tastes. All four of us are into food. Jess and I love cookies. His love of cookies shows the playful side of him that intrigues. They have this wonderfully huge pantry, like the pantries of my childhood where one could walk down and smoked meat would hang from the ceiling and bushel baskets of goodies would be everywhere. The shelves in their pantry are always lined with sacks of cookies. I know one should use the proper word bag but I love the word sack which is what we say in the south. It's got an earthy intimate sound.

Robert begins to be sick just when my life with Mack becomes utterly unbearable. It's hard to share with them our problems. No matter how much I love them, this relationship is Mack's terrain. I am the invited guest, welcome but not loved as Mack is loved. His connection makes this closeness possible. I want to say or do nothing that changes how Robert sees him. It is more than obvious that Robert who truly identifies only with the mythic feminine will always choose the phallic bond over a relationship with a flesh and blood female any day. This does not pain me. I fret about losing my connection to Jess—whom I love, who always makes me feel loved.

Everything changes when Robert begins to be sick. Suddenly, we no longer see him as the eternal one in our midst. Suddenly our times together seem more like a gift. Now and then we do some routine thing together like take him to and fro, to the doctor, to the hospital for his kidney stuff. Suddenly he is less this mysterious, gifted poet and more a frail aging queen who like the rest of us is afraid of dying and leaving all that he loves best.

Robert will never understand my longing to leave Mack. He will always see me in a bad light. He just does not know that the image Mack offers him to see is made up of those parts that have already turned from lead into gold. The poisonous parts Robert will never know. He can imagine Mack suffering at the hands of the demonic feminine but never know my pain.

For a long time she assumed Mack was as enchanted as she was with the idea of an aesthetics of existence. She has trouble seeing that he is most passionate about autonomy, that it is her energy which fills the space of their life with an aesthetic wholeness. He has a few primary passions— poetry, sex, music—and rarely moves beyond them into other worlds. Because he goes along with her dreams and schemes she can't see that it is just that—a humoring of her whims and not a sharing. Mack appropriates but he does not share. There is nothing she gives him that he does not feel another woman cannot replace.

Jess says little when things begin to go wrong between her and Mack, only that she must not be hurt. While he will not take sides it's clear he understands all the things in Mack's nature Duncan refuses to see. It comforts her to know he understands and cares. Yet, she never tries to tell him what is going wrong, not even when he offers to listen.

When things go wrong between her and Mack, she thinks all the more about Robert and Jess, about what has made their life work for the more than thirty years they have been together. It must have helped that they met when they were both grown people, artists, who had made clear choices about how they wanted to live in the world. She loved to hear them talk about the early days when they first met and began to make a life together. A devotion to art was their common center. Sometimes she thinks that what comes between her and Mack is that they are busy trying to have jobs in the real world, the way interactions there change the nature of how they relate to one another.

Since the very beginning, it has felt like Mack and I are leading two lives—one as artists trying to create a body of work and the other as individuals striving to make academic careers. In that world everyone gets pitted against one another. No wonder then that from the beginning academics have wanted to know don't we find it difficult, both of us being poets, being writers. Yet that's not where the separation and conflict occur. It's the shared longing to be fulfilled in the art and act of creating work that binds us.

Those moments where we share in art together, whether it is the pleasures of Rumi's texts (like Robert we too are obsessed with Rumi) or hearing him read, this is our place of hope and certainty, of beauty and light. This is the place where our spirits commune, where we can hear with shared delight the noises of the soul in play. Like us, Robert feels this delight. We warm to the excitement in his voice when he says: You must hear this new poem. It stays with me—the opening lines: *The child I was has been left behind. Those who first loved me have gone on without me. Where they were a door has been left open upon a solitude. In the midst of our revelry I find myself waiting.*

32

Male possession of women's bodies is central to the maintenance of patriarchy. Even in my teens I believed that women with men would be free if we embraced non-monogamy. If men did not see us as their "belongings" it would make it easier for them to respect our assertion of subjectivity. In my life that has been the case. Even though lots of our friends looked at our relationship and felt it was doomed the moment I was involved with another man. Note: no one felt his involvements with other women doomed the relationship. I never see our relationship as doomed. Even at the worst moments of crisis we try to work things through. To me and to Mack the value of our relationship is defined not by whether we stay together but by whether we are loving toward one another. We talk all the time about being friends if the time comes when we need to part.

• • •

She thinks he can be friends. Even though he's not main-
tained any friendships with ex-girlfriends. Her belief in
the power of love to transform everything is so strong;
it blinds her to reality. She has coped with his lovers and
ex-lovers with openheartedness, but he has always alter-
nated between acceptance and punishment.

He thinks that I would never leave him but that's not so. I
just want to know that before I leave, I have done everything possible to try and make our life work. I don't want
to leave with bitterness. After my exams are done, I am
more understanding about his relationship with Tina. She
really sounds like she is more his soul mate than I could
ever be. I alternate between feeling happiness for him
that he has found a love that opens him up more—that
makes him tender, generous, expansive—and my anger
that he springs this on me just at the time that I need his
support. That's what I feel he does all the time these
days—pull the carpet from under me. Lately I feel this
constant sense of anxiety, as though our life together has
become a minefield—it's never clear when a bomb will
explode. The one thing that I know to be certain is that I
have a dissertation to write.

When explosions happen too often, I leave. I go to live
with Betty and her British lover, Susan, the lesbian
couple I stay with on nights that I commute to San
Francisco. Betty thinks I should leave, that I can't see

how jealous Mack is of me, the way he does everything he can to hold me back. I'm only in their place for a few days before Susan expresses jealousy about the time Betty and I spend together, the long hours we spend hanging out in the bathroom, soaking in the tub. I can't stay with them. I don't know I have left the house I live in—Mack should leave. I return home. He's pissed, but I don't care. I state clearly and definitively I have a dissertation to write. After that we can talk about the future. And while I am writing it he can do whatever he wants to do.

I came home because when I left women just seemed to come out of the woodwork telling me about how something bizarre happened in their relationships with men—husbands and lovers—right before their Ph.D. exams or while they were doing dissertations. A lot of them were abandoned just when they finished the exams. Some of them never wrote their dissertations or took years to write them. What stuns most is the bitterness that remains even though many of them ended these relationships ages ago. I don't want this to happen to me. I go home to sit in my study, in the beautiful home that I made with the sound of the ocean, pink azaleas, and the smell of eucalyptus outside my window. I go home to write. That's what I do. Life calms down again. Mack and I return to living in the bittersweet peace and calm we have always known. All the anger gone. It's damaged us though. There are lines in a relationship that once crossed make it hard to go back. We have everything back except the desire I always felt for him.

When I finish my dissertation we talk about the next step in our life. He tells me that he still loves Tina, that he dreams of being with her, that even though he's told me that he broke contact, they've been writing and talking. I'm done with anger. I urge him to go and see her, to find out where this is leading—that more than anything I want to love him in a way that nurtures his well-being. I don't want him to stay with me if he loves Tina so much and believes they can have a good life together. While I urge him to go, I also tell him honestly that I can't be sure that I will be here when he returns. For the first time in our life I am having a fling. My new lover is younger than me—Jamaican—a pretty party boy. We are just into having fun.

Tina and Mack meet in New York. He calls me from the hotel room to talk. I speak with Tina. It's not the first time. We talked for hours when their relationship first began. We plan to meet—the three of us. While Mack is gone, I spend time with Edward. We like to play together. We are always eating. I like it that we are not that into sex. It's fun the sex but it's not what brings us together. More and more it's making him grumpy that it is clear I have no intention of changing my life with Mack. They run into each other from time to time, speak but say little else. This bothers Edward. Men have trouble being the third party. Even when a couple chooses non-monogamy men still have the upper hand. It's still better to have a committed open relationship. Especially so if you start living with somebody young like

I did. And all those people we know who married young are having the worst time.

Things are good when Mack comes. He and Tina have decided to just be close friends. She's still more the love of his life than I am. That doesn't make me sad; I like to see Mack recovering lost parts of himself. This is what openness means, letting each other have the space to grow.

She wants him to grow, to be fully self-actualized. That's the language she used that he laughs at. All that religious self-help nonsense annoys him. He really thinks it's all shit but he knows there's no point in telling her that. After all that time, all the mess they've been through he can't believe she is still such a fucking innocent. It was the eternal openness in her that he loved in the beginning— that still attracts him even though he wants to crush her spirit.

I apply for a job as an assistant professor at Yale University. I can see that Mack does not think I have a chance to get this job. He probably thinks I'm not good enough— too unconventional. He's supportive, says even that if I get the job he will take a year off and come with me. New Haven seems like a horrible place to live and Yale a horrible place to work. We both know that Santa Cruz will never hire me even though they say I can return once I prove myself somewhere else. My white feminist dissertation adviser tells me not to wear the color red and not to wear my hair in braids when I go to my job interview. I know she wants me to succeed. She thinks I need to try and behave more professionally. I know I've got to be who I am or Yale will not be the place for me.

I refuse to go to the job convention to be interviewed. Mack thinks I'm crazy, already rebelling. My logic is simply that I don't have the money to go all the way back east to interview for a job I might not get. If I am one of their top candidates—and maybe even the top one—I'll know because they will find a way to bring me to New Haven. And they do.

New Haven is such a bleak sad city. An abandoned black city in America. My interview sucks. It does not matter that my hair is braided or that I wore my heavy red sweater. It's the only sweater I have. I am not about to freeze to death so as not to be wearing red. Poor me. I'm fucking hopeless. When that man was so arrogant and nasty at the interview, that light-skinned Caribbean black man, I met him toe to toe, letting him know that if you fuck with me, I'll fuck with you right back. All the while I'm thinking to myself You are really making a mess of this. I'm just glad when it's over and I can get out of the snow and go home to sunshine, azaleas, and eucalyptus.

When she first came home she was all sure she had fucked up the interview and didn't get the job. Mack was all Mr. Nice Nice and Comfort Comfort. When the calls come from the historian in African American studies with the sexy voice telling her she's got the job, Mack is with-

drawn. She accepts without pause having made up her mind that it's time for her to take care of business, to find out whether the academy is for her or not. Suddenly, Mack forgets all about saying he will go with her. Maybe now she will see him as he really is.

I can't believe it. We talked about it. Right here in this yellow kitchen, we talked about it. And I was told that he would take a leave for a year and come with me. I'm sure that's what Mack said. I heard him say it.

Just as though he has not heard a word she says he goes right on with the mindfuck, telling her she must be confused, she must have misheard. Telling her, he doesn't even know if he can get a leave, that he could not possibly have promised her to go with her. It was just like the day that first book of hers came. He just pissed on her success right then. That was the phrase she had used in all that therapy that didn't go anywhere. If it had he wouldn't be treating her this way now. She's really confused. She really wants to believe that she misheard him.

When I first talked to Mack about the job, he was supportive and was willing to go. I was too thrilled and told Beverly, my girlfriend in Atlanta. Since all my girlfriends and I had been talking about whether or not Mack would be able to handle me getting a job at a prestigious school I wanted to wave the banner of triumph in their faces. He had come through for me. Now I have to call Beverly and

251

ask her to repeat what I told her the other night. She repeats exactly what I think I've heard. That's when it is clear he's just pissing on my success. Now I know I have to leave Mack. That he is not ready for me to grow. I tell him in a straightforward manner: I plan to take this job and move to New Haven whether you are going or not. He tells me he needs to think about it. Waiting for his response fills me with such anxiety. It terrorizes me. I don't really believe I can go without Mack. I can't leave this house that I love—that is my first and only true home.

He tells me later, his voice full of complaints, that he doesn't want to come but he will—that he has found out about the leave and it's fine. We talk about it in that calm way that we have always used to talk about things. It's too late though. I don't want him to come. He's crushed my small moments of triumph, pissed all over my successes again and again. It's no good. Somehow he's still trying to keep me the dependent country child-woman he fell for who was unsure and desperate for him to save her life. It's breaking my heart to think about leaving Mack. I came into this life thinking that he was my savior and my rescuer. Now I have to see how much parts of him want to destroy me. I have tried not to face those parts, to hold on to the hope that we could work everything out. I don't have any more hope.

When I tell mama that I am planning to leave Mack, she not only expresses disbelief she tells me that would be *the stupidest thing you have ever done.* And even my closest friend tells me *You are making a mistake, good men are hard to find out here, shit you do anything you want and Mack is fine with that—girl you better stay your ass where you are.* It's funny. Only my lesbian girl-friends and Marijke let me know that I am doing the right thing. Marijke was the first woman in our feminist group to leave her husband over political differences. She was tired of her man acting like women's politics don't matter. In lots of ways I think it's politics that's pulling me and Mack apart, the politics of academe where competition is the norm; the politics of race in white supremacy where a black man and a black woman are constantly pitted against one another; the politics of gender where I want to grow, be free, be my own woman and he is afraid of that. Anyhow mama says she will not even waste her time talking with me about it, because she does not believe I am going anywhere by myself.

Mack and I go about our lives just as though there is no plan for me to leave. Maybe I'll change my mind. Maybe he will come with me. That's not what I feel though. In my heart I feel it's time for us to part. We don't tell anyone around us that we are going separate ways. Maybe because we are not sure. Sometimes I lie in the bed at night sure that I am making a mistake. All those horrible times when everything was fucked up and I went nowhere, and now everything is calm and peaceful and I am choosing to leave.

Betty is thrilled. She thinks I will blossom without Mack. She tells me that she can't wait to get the report cause she knows my life will change in ways that I could never imagine. She keeps insisting *Girl, he's been holding you back*. I don't think Mack has been holding me back. It's true that lots of times when I could have been doing other things, I was preoccupied with the mess this relationship was in. But I was part of that mess. And it was my job as well as his to help clean it up.

When I tell a few folks that I will be leaving for good, they don't believe it. They think Mack and I have had an ideal relationship, two intellectual artistic black people making a life together. Sometimes it scares me, cause it does seem that our relationship, even with the really awful problems, is still more solid, more together than those of most of the folks we know. My best girlfriends are puzzled. Why now—when you guys have weathered the storms and are finally reaching dry land.

It's hard to explain to anybody. It's hard to tell them what I see when I look deep inside Mack's heart. I see there a place where he hates me. And the me that he hates is the woman I have become. He keeps looking back with longing for the child-woman I was when we met. He keeps looking back to the promise that I will be the balm to soothe the wounds of childhood. And instead all the remembered hurts linger, and something about being with me makes the pain more intense.

Mack went to a black woman therapist once. He spent the first visits ranting and raving about me. Therapy was fine. But the moment she told him that it was time for him to talk about himself, about his pain, he left and never went back. I have been a scapegoat, his and everyone else's. That was my role in the family. After all I did not go far from them. My sisters were right. I can see that now.

It's bittersweet. Cause there are so many ways in which Mack is not like my family. He has nurtured my intellectual growth. When no one else was affirming that I could write my books he was there. Nothing can change that. All these years that's been my fear—that if I leave him, I will not be able to write. Nothing can change the fact that in this life I became a writer, in the calm contemplative sanctuary of a home where the heartbeat of life is words.

I can't tell anyone how afraid I feel. Sometimes there is this voice within that whispers to me: *You are gonna go mad, you know, if you leave him. You won't be able to hold it together.* Sometimes even that voice says You'll die. I'm not afraid of dying, I am afraid of not becoming the writer I want to be.

33

We had not been sleeping together for weeks. I lie awake
at night trying to imagine my life without him. I don't
want to leave Mack, I want to leave behind a life where I
am punished for speaking my mind. In all ways I want to
grow up. I entered this life just before I turned twenty
and now I am closer to forty—not close enough to make
this my midlife crisis, but close enough to make me see
that it is time to change. I hate it when feminist friends
try to make Mack the enemy. They hear my pain—hear
me tell my story—but he has his story. Like pieces of a
puzzle that look the same but don't fit, our stories don't
match. In his story I am the terrorist—the demanding
one whose needs he could never satisfy. I have never pretended to be undemanding. I have never pretended that
I have not caused him pain.

He reads me lines from a Duncan poem he believes

describes my behavior—the way I pick at things until they fall apart: *i was moved by violent conflicts and yearnings. a need to be reassured in love that all but obscured any act of loving.* It is a rare moment of utter agreement between us. I am intimate with the sound of my own pain.

Everyone wants me to be angry with Mack, to blame him, for me not to just pack my car with things I can't leave behind. Most of me stays. My clothes hang in the atticlike closets, everything neat and tidy on my desk, the handmade Japanese plates still on the shelf. Most of my books have not been packed. I need to leave as though I am only departing for a while, as though any day now I will return. I am not angry. In *The Bluest Eye*, my favorite book—the first one I pack—Morrison writes: *Anger is better. There is a presence in anger.* She's right. But I have never been a girl for anger. Grief is my chosen passion. I am sad. That's why Mack has always seen me as a mourner at the heartbreak church—our witty invented imaginary location—the place where grief is the order of the day.

If the world were not moved by grief, there would be no poetry. For it is suffering that brings us closer to the gods. Poetry brought us together and keeps us together still. I can never leave Mack for parts of him have become parts of me, our spirits shaped by the poetics of a life in words. We are each other's fate.

34

Now I too am a "high plains drifter" searching the road for my destiny, intent upon living in a world where there is no looking back. No matter that I have left a field of shattered dreams behind me. I am carrying my one true dream inside. It has been loaded in the car like all the small necessary possessions of life. Clint Eastwood movies appear before me as I drive. It is only in westerns that I have seen the frontier—the Great Plains. Now we will meet face to face. In the movies, the Eastwood movies I love so much, I am the silent stranger who enters a town and leaves it changed—a trail of bodies in my wake.

The bodies he leaves behind like stigmata. In *High Plains Drifter* the mournful cowboy cannot rest. He kills to avenge and loose the hold passion has on his spirit. True outlaws are gripped by passion, held sway by its torments. The renegade cowboy rides in search of freedom. He is never compelled by dreams of conquest. He is a man of heart who follows the call of all wild murmurings—the wildest of which is sorrow. My sorrow is so great it breaks me.

On a clear bright morning I leave behind California blue sky, the bluest sky that I have ever seen. The redwoods, the sand, the ocean, all are places where bits and pieces of my heart seem scattered. I am driving toward the frontier—moving toward desert and wasteland. The frontier was found and quickly destroyed. The Great Plains is still reeling from the sorrow of everything that happened there. Buffalo are stuck in a place of memory where even the ones that live to stand as testimony wear only a thick hide of remembered slaughter. There is no place left to go—no place to flee.

Wherever I go I take with me all the accumulated words, the stories that haunt me, that come back again and again to remind me of who I might have been if indeed it was not possible to change the direction of stories. Even though I want to be a writer I don't want to change my life. Still I don't want to make the heartbreak church my home. I never believed writers have to know heartbreak to give us a true story of passion. Even so suffering changes me. I wonder sometimes about Emily Dickinson's suffering alone in her house of words, alone in her dreams. Just like death we can't keep suffering away.

Driving toward the desert I enter a landscape of

wounds. When I was a child I heard again and again how our savior went into the desert to find his life again. Into the desert he fled with his heartache and his unrequited love. When he reappeared from his longest journey, to the desert only he had seen, the wasteland of the cross and death hanging there, he was recognized, known only by the wounds of passion imprinted on his hands. My favorite saint, Teresa of Avila, wanted to share his wounds, for him to give her what she called *a taste of this love*, so he pierced her with a golden dart. Stigmata were her witness and her testimony. Somewhere when we have come to the end of our journey, when we are no longer mourners at the heartbreak church, when we no longer feel that there is anything that stands between us and all that we have been seeking, our confession will be simply that there was never any witness. The story was written so that it could stand alone, two hands raised to glory, that the spirit may descend among us, one hand raised to glory, that the spirit has come—touched me and left my body whole.

CPSIA information can be obtained
at www.ICGtesting.com
Printed in the USA
LVHW041132100522
718380LV00003B/451

9 780805 057225